WORKPLACE BASICS
with ESOL EXERCISES

Book 1 from DTR Inc.'s Work Readiness & ESOL Training Series

Student Book

JAY GOLDBERG

The opinions expressed in this manuscript are solely the opinions of the author and do not represent the opinions or thoughts of the publisher.

This book was written to help individuals understand and improve their employability knowledge and skills. The information detailed in the book is based on the experience, knowledge and observations of Jay Goldberg. Since hiring, firing, and promoting employees varies by company and the person performing the task, there is no guarantee by the author or publisher, expressed or implied that following everything in this book will result in a job, not getting fired, or an increase in compensation; or that employees that read this book will implement what they learn and become exceptional employees.

Business Consulting, Mentoring & Workplace Training Development

Contact the author, via email, at Book@DTRConsulting.BIZ. Please type "your work readiness ESOL book" in the subject line of the email to ensure that your email is not deleted as junk mail.

To order more books go to www.createspace.com/5972341

Business web site: www.DTRConsulting.BIZ

ISBN: 978-1523206582

Table of Contents

IMPORTANT NOTE TO STUDENTS:

This four book work readiness/ESOL series (the current plan is to have all four books available by the end of 2016 at the latest) has worksheets and exercises for both the work readiness topics covered in the book (in this case workplace basics) and for ESOL topics (such as reading, writing, grammar, speaking & listening, career, and technical). Some of the work readiness exercises meet requirements for both work readiness and ESOL competencies.

The work readiness topics, worksheets and exercises in this edition of the book are **exactly the same** as in the non-ESOL version of the book. Employers do not have different workplace expectations or requirements for employees enrolled in (or who graduated from) ESOL programs. In addition, ESOL students want and deserve the same opportunities as anyone else to excel and grow at work. To ensure this, the work readiness portion in **any** ESOL program needs to be exactly the same as a work readiness program for non-ESOL participants.

Only work readiness topics are covered in the **text** of the book. It is assumed that ESOL/ESL programs already have materials to teach topics such as reading, writing, grammar, etc.

Therefore, the ESOL exercises in this book are used to apply those previously taught and learned skills to workplace materials and situations; and to further help the participants understand the work readiness topics taught in Workplace Basics.

Since the work readiness materials are the same as the ones for non-ESOL participants; these materials are targeting high-middle tier to upper tier ESOL students.

NOTE - if your ESOL program is currently using work readiness materials; please make sure that it is not a specialized, watered-down version for ESOL which, as stated above, is not ideal. Remember, unlike the reading, writing, grammar, etc. portion of ESOL courses where the participant/student is the main client for the course; in work readiness courses, employers are the main clients, not the participants/students. This is because the employers will eventually decide how successful the participants are; not assessments or instructors. So work readiness courses, ESOL included, have to "graduate" participants/students that posses what employers expect and need. If any other criteria are used, there is a significant risk that the workplace will not place any value in the work readiness credential obtained by the "graduates" of that program.

Work Readiness Series with ESOL exercises by Jay Goldberg (all available sometime in 2016)

Workplace Basics with ESOL Exercises (classroom and instructor books)
Workplace Skills with ESOL Exercises (classroom and instructor books)
People Skills with ESOL Exercises (classroom and instructor books)
Customer Service with ESOL Exercises (classroom and instructor books)

Program Prep

ESOL Classroom Program Success Measurement Worksheet

How has your success in the ESOL program you are enrolled in been measured so far? List as many ways as you can think of.

_____

_____

_____

_____

_____

_____

ESOL Workplace Success Measurement Worksheet

How do you believe your success will be measured on the job? Keep in mind that performing your specific job functions is just one of the job activities you will be held accountable for. You also have to be a "good employee."

_____

_____

_____

_____

_____

_____

_____

ESOL EXERCISE PREP 1

Q1. When called on, explain to the class the workplace success measurement topics indicated in the Workplace Success Measurement Worksheet above that need to be included in the success measurements for this ESOL work readiness course to improve the course. The goal is to be measured, at least in large part, as you will be measured on the job so you know what to expect on the job and so you can work on areas where you need improvement before you start your job.

Q2. Demonstrate means clearly showing the existence or truth of (something) by giving proof or evidence. Competency means the ability to do something successfully or efficiently. Therefore, if you pass demonstrated competencies in a course or training program; what does that mean?

    A. That you have not proved you can do something successfully
    B. That you have proved you can do something successfully
    C. That no conclusion can be reached on whether or not you proved that you can do something successfully
    D. That you have not been given the opportunity to either prove or not prove that you can do something.

*****

ESOL EXERCISE PREP 2

Write a three paragraph essay explaining what the term "workplace basics" means to you. The first paragraph should introduce the topic (purpose of the three paragraph write-up) and contain a couple of sentences regarding your definition of "workplace basics." The second paragraph should contain some specific behaviors and or skills that help illustrate your definition (what an employee needs to do to ensure that he or she performs "workplace basics" up to the standards of his or her supervisor). The third paragraph should have a conclusion regarding why workplace basics are important to employers.

_____

_____

_____

_____

_____

_____

_____

_____

_____

_____

_____

_____

_____

_____

The Profit Motive of Business

In the National Football League (NFL), the amount of money set aside for employee salaries (players) is a set percentage of **revenue** earned by the owners. The more money earned by the League, from ticket sales, television contracts, etc., the more money the players make. The contract negotiated between the owners and players clearly shows the relationship between the business and its employees. If the league negotiates more money from the television networks, player salaries rise. If NFL games suddenly do poorly in the ratings, and the league gets less money in its television contracts, player salaries decline. If the league suddenly could not get any television contracts, employees could lose their jobs (player rosters could be cut).

While most businesses do not have a negotiated rate of revenue which they use on employee wages, the concept is the same. The more money a business makes, the more money it has to spend on employee salaries and benefits, and the less likely it is to have layoffs (employees lose their jobs).

Therefore, you are similar to an NFL player. Your team is the business that hires you. Your game is your day to day job. Your opposition is businesses that sell similar products and services, and/or businesses that are after the same pot of money and customers that your business serves but sells different product or services.

For example, if you work for the consumer electronics company Best Buy and listen closely you can hear the game announcer saying: "Starting for the Best Buy Giants at Senior Sales Representative, is Jay Goldberg. Goldberg is on a twenty day streak of generating sales revenue of over $20,000 a day. Goldberg's run has moved Best Buy into first place, just ahead of the BrandsMart Cowboys. It has also kicked in his sales bonus making Goldberg one of the highest paid salesmen in his field. Perhaps best of all, unbeknownst to Goldberg, his recent sales streak has allowed Best Buy management to keep John Doe on full time. Without the extra revenue earned by Goldberg, Doe's hours would have been cut and he would have had trouble earning enough money to pay his rent, which would have created a difficult situation for him, his wife, and two children."

The paragraph above was written to show a fun example. I have no knowledge about the compensation structure, or sales goals of Best Buy or any other consumer electronics company. I have also bought and been a satisfied customer of both Best Buy and BrandsMart and having Best Buy win the above competition in no way indicates that I prefer Best Buy to BrandsMart.

Q1. What is the meaning of the word "revenue" (typed in bold) in the first paragraph on the previous page?

    A. All the money earned by owners from normal business activities (in this case from the football teams) minus all the expenses the owners spend on normal business activities (in this case from the football teams).

    B. All the money earned by the business owner(s) whether from the business (in this case from the football teams), investments or side businesses (in this case, businesses other than from the football teams).

    C. All the money earned by the business owner for normal business operations (in this case from the football teams).

    D. All the money spent by the owners during normal business activities (in this case from the football teams).

Q2. What is the author's purpose in providing the example of how the National Football League (NFL) operates?

    A. To teach people about the National Football League (NFL) because it is the most popular sport in the United States.

    B. To provide an example on why it should be important to employees (workers) that the business they work for makes money (profits).

    C. To show how salary negotiations work between employers and employees.

    D. To let readers know that if they like football, they should watch all the games they can to help support the players so they can make good money (salaries).

Q3. Past Perfect Tense indicates that an action was completed (finished or "perfected") at some point in the past before something else happened. Which sentence below is past perfect tense?

    A. The contract between the players and owners allow both the owners and players to keep earning money.

    B. The contract between players and owners was signed.

    C. The contract between players and owners was negotiated before games were played.

    D. None of the above.

Q4. Past Participle indicates a prior or completed action (or time). Which sentence below is a past participle?

    A. The contract between the players and owners allow both the owners and players to keep earning money.

    B. The contract between players and owners was signed.

    C. The contract between players and owners was negotiated before games were played.

    D. None of the above.

Q5. Present Participle refers to action that is happening at the time of speaking. Which sentence below is present participle?

    A. The contract between the players and owners allow the both the owners and players to keep earning money.
    B. The contract between players and owners was signed.
    C. The contract between players and owners was negotiated before games were played.
    D. None of the above.

*****

Another old "wise" tale I heard from an old wise man at a meeting; in my days generating a work readiness program and curriculum for a South Florida client, follows.

The owner of a small manufacturing firm in Florida called his entire staff together for a meeting. Everyone knew the meeting was about the status of a pending contract. The manufacturing company had worked on previous contracts for the company for whom it was awaiting word on a new contract. In the past, contracts with this company resulted in a lot of highly stressful work, which included long hours and tight timeframes for product delivery. The owner then announced that the company did <u>not</u> get the contract. There were cheers all around the room because workers were relieved that they would not have to go through the long days and stressful times again. The next day many started being fired from their jobs. Without that client, the manufacturing company did not have the funds to keep everyone employed.

Your job is available because the company that employs you is conducting enough business, and making enough money, for that job to be needed. Therefore, your job and associated pay scale are tied directly to the success of the business you work for. In addition, one of the best ways for your pay to increase is to stay with the same company for at least two or three years to show that employer or potential future employers that you have both the ability to commit to a company, and have gained the experience and knowledge to take on a job with more responsibilities at higher pay. Therefore, it is very important to you that the business you work for is profitable so you can keep your job, improve your resume, and grow your earnings, instead of continually jumping sideways.

As a final exercise, let's assume you are the owner of a small business. Five years ago you took a $75,000 loan to start up the business and used the equity in your home as collateral. Over the past five years you have struggled to grow the business, putting most of the money you earned back into the business. In doing so, your credit card debt has grown to $25,000. Now, in year five, your sales have exploded. You are able to finally take a good salary, start significantly paying down your debt and can hire a three person sales force and a full time customer service representative. What has to happen for you to keep those four people employed?   <insert 30 seconds of game show music here>

The answer is that the money brought in by the three salespeople has to at least cover the money you are paying the four of them (including benefits, taxes, and their overhead).

Let's say in year one, the three salespeople bring in enough to cover all their expenses plus 10%. You decide to split the 10% profit with your employees by using half of those profits to increase their base pay. Now, in year two the three salespeople come up 20% short of all the money it costs you to employ them. That 20% shortfall comes out of your pocket. That was money you were using to help pay down your credit card and home loans. However, your employees still expect a raise. If you give them a raise and they have the same year next year that they did in year two, the money you earn will go down even more.

Now you're thinking that you took the risk to start the business; you are the person in debt because of the business; so why should you be the one whose earnings go down while everyone else's salary goes up?

You would not be wrong, but business owners also realize that if the business does well, they stand to profit more than their employees (deservingly so since the owners take the risks).

Therefore, you decide that you'll take a hit and reward your best employees, but you won't take the full hit. You decide to give raises to your two top salespeople and your customer service representative. You also fire your worst salesperson and split his/her work amongst the other two salespeople, feeling no guilt since they are getting raises, while, you the owner, are taking less compensation. You also have a plan in place to cut back the hours for the customer service representative if the two salespeople do not show improvement over last year's sales volume within four months.

See - if you were an owner, the amount of money you pay your employees, and how many employees you hire would depend upon the profits your business was making. After all you took the risk, you deserve a salary, and you have bills to pay.

In this example, the owner could have easily decided to fire the salesperson with the least time in the business, or the salesperson that the owner did not get along with, if the sales results were fairly even, or if the owner believed that the remaining sales people could improve. Workers livelihoods are directly tied to the success of the business with whom they are employed.

The above example works for large businesses and chains as well as small businesses. Owners still base jobs and worker's pay on the profitability of the business. For company-owned chain stores, store managers' compensation (and job security) is often tied to the profitability of the store he/she is managing.

ESOL EXERCISE WB2

Q1. What is the main idea of this chapter?

_____

_____

Q2. List three examples used in the chapter to help the reader understand the main idea.

    1. _____

    2. _____

    3. _____

Q3. Remember this passage: "See - if you were an owner, the amount of money you pay your employees, and how many employees you hire would depend upon the profits your business was making. After all you took the risk, you deserve a salary, and you have bills to pay."

Is this a fact or an opinion? _____

Why did you choose your answer?

_____

_____

Q4. In the chapter the phrase old "wise" tale is used with quotes around the word wise. This is a play on words from the phrase old wives' tale. An old wives tale is used to indicate that a supposed truth is actually a superstition or something untrue, to be ridiculed.

Q4A. Why do you think the author did not use the common, known phrase old wives' tale?

_____

_____

_____

_____

Q4B. Why do you think the author put quotes around the word wise; and why do you think he choose the word wise?

_____

_____

_____

_____

*****

EXERCISE WB1

You are running a 27 week, 10 team, 50 years old plus outdoor basketball league. All teams play each other three times. Each team supplies its own coach and there are two refs per game. There are no playoffs. If teams tie for first, the winner of the head-to-head series between the teams is crowned the winner of the league. All 12 members of the winning team get a trophy. The league supplies uniforms for all team members.

Q1. How many people will you need to hire? _____

Q2. List all the expenses that might be involved, including staff expenses.

_____
_____
_____
_____
_____
_____
_____
_____
_____
_____
_____

Q3. How much do you think you can charge each team? _____

Q4. Total up all your expenses. _____

Q5. Calculate your revenue (# of players times what you are charging each player).

players _____ price charging _____ total revenue _____

Q6. Since the main goal for every business is to make profits; is the league profitable?

NOTE: Profits = Revenue minus Expenses   Yes it is profitable   No it in NOT profitable

Q7. What other factors could impact profits plus or minus?

_____
_____
_____
_____
_____
_____
_____
_____
_____

*****

Time Is Money

Pink Floyd's classic album, *Dark Side of the Moon* contains songs titled "Time" and "Money." Many consider this album one of the best rock albums ever. Certainly, I do. So did Pink Floyd subconsciously incorporate these two keys as songs on their album to assure its success? Perhaps. Or maybe the cosmos rewarded them for discovering this successful workplace connection. Hmmm. Or maybe they're just very talented and I'm pointing out random facts to help introduce this topic. Actually, that sounds about right.

Absenteeism

When an employee takes off from work unexpectedly, the amount of work that has to be completed on the job doesn't change. That means the co-workers of the employee that misses work, now have more work to do. So workers that make a habit of missing days due to illness or personal problems that need to be taken care of during work hours are <u>not</u> popular with their co-workers. It doesn't matter why. Whether for car problems, day care problems, a hang nail, etc., co-workers will be annoyed with people who do not show up to work when scheduled for work. If a worker doesn't show up because his/her day care provider cancelled, co-workers aren't going to say, "No problem, you do what you have to. I don't mind not being able to go on even a bathroom break today because your day care provider didn't show up." It's more likely that your co-workers (who are more like friendly neighbors than tried and true friends) will say, "Great, I have to suffer because that a*****e doesn't have a backup plan in place in case of emergencies. Here I am living with no air conditioning for two days so I can wait until a day off to have a repair person come over and fix it so I won't miss work, and now I have to have a tough day because my co-worker didn't show up."

But that's not the worst of it. That worker's supervisor will now have to help out to get the work completed. After all, that supervisor is being paid to assure all work is completed successfully; work he or she normally does, and work done by his or her staff. In fact, the supervisor may have to stay late to finish the additional work. And most supervisors are on salary, not a per hour rate so they do not get overtime pay.

Now keep in mind that this supervisor is the person who determines employee raises; keeps that worker and others employed, and recommends employees for promotions. Therefore inconveniencing the supervisor who will now have to do his or her normal work plus help out performing additional work to make up for the absent employee, is not the ideal career move.

So how happy do you think supervisors are with employees who do not show up to work on their scheduled days? If you were a supervisor, how pleased would you be? So absenteeism has a negative impact on your co-workers and supervisor.

In addition, all companies have policies on absenteeism. Therefore, not staying within those work rules comes with consequences. Excessive absenteeism is grounds for being fired. And being fired leaves a big hole in one's resume when he or she looks for their next job.

Use of sick days

Please be aware that in trying to be fair to employees many companies allow a generous amount of sick days. Often the longer you work for a company, the more sick days you earn.

Sick days are not vacation days or even personal days. They are an insurance policy the company provides to its employees. They are to be used only when an employee is sick. Since sick days are an unplanned absence, when used there is a negative impact on the workplace. If all employees used all their sick days a company would have no choice but to reduce sick days for everyone. Think how high your car insurance would be if every driver except you had two accidents a year. Insurance companies cannot pay out money it does not have. They cannot survive if they pay out more money than they take in. No business could. In this case everyone's car insurance rates would go up (including yours) to an amount where the insurance company was taking in more money than it was paying out.

Therefore, employees who abuse their sick days are hurting their co-workers. That makes that employee someone that the workplace would be better off without.

Let's say that Jane Doe has worked for the business for ten years and has used only 10 sick days during that time. Furthermore, during that time Jane has accrued (built up a backlog of) 50 sick days. Then she gets very sick and will have to be hospitalized for three weeks and stay in bed at home for an additional three weeks. This means she will miss 30 days. This is exactly what the sick days were provided to Jane Doe for. She will be paid for missing the 6 weeks of work because of the company's sick days (insurance) policy. This situation is also more controllable for the business. Knowing the amount of time that Jane Doe will be out, the company can hire a temp to help out, or build in a little time delay in delivering products/services when talking to customers. If these 30 days were used at random during that 10 year span, the company would not have been able to bring in a temp, and would not have known to build in time delays when talking to customers.

Now, let's look at a company where employees were misusing sick days. In order to curb the misuse, the company decides to cut the number of sick days allowed in half. Therefore, Jane Doe has earned 30 total sick days instead of 60 (50 backlog plus 10 she used). Since she used 10 sick days, Jane Doe only has 20 sick days left to cover her six week absence (30 days). Jane Doe's illness, therefore, would have resulted in her being out of work for 10 days (2 weeks) without pay. The result could be that she gets behind in her rent, never gets caught up, and either has to move or gets evicted.

Workers who abuse sick days are certainly hurting the company, hurting their co-workers, and hurting their supervisor.

Here is a final car insurance, sick day analogy. You pay for car insurance and if you do not get into an accident you do not get your money back from the insurance company. You pay for insurance in case you need it. In fact, insurance is the ultimate good neighbor product because you not getting into accidents meant that some of the money you paid for the insurance went to help other people who got into accidents (the money has to come from somewhere). Sick days are exactly the same. If you do not get sick you do not earn any money for days that go unused. However, it means that the company can have a good sick day policy to help employees who need to use them. And one day that just may be you.

Finally, if you use your full allotment of sick days because you have a lot of one day illnesses, your job could be in jeopardy. In the National Football League (NFL), a player that gets injured often may find it difficult to stick with a team. If a team cannot count on that player being available on game day, his roster spot could go to a lesser player who that team can rely on. It is no different in business. If a company is relying on five people to man the phones for calls from customers, and often comes up short because "a player" is on the "injured list" (one specific employee is often out sick), the supervisor could fire that employee (cut the player) who is the cause of the company losing customers and money because the company is constantly operating "one man down" (only four people on the phones).

Tardiness

By now you should have a good idea of what I am going to say about showing up late for work, extending lunches, and extending breaks. If you are tardy you are not only a "bad workplace neighbor", but quite frankly, a bad employee.

A lot of thought and analysis goes into creating work schedules. Often department A cannot start its work until department B completes its work. Other times, in order to meet customer expectations, to satisfy and keep those customers, work must be completed within specific timeframes.

Tardiness is the villain of both of these situations. If you show up 30 minutes late and do a phenomenal job, but that meant that the company had people sitting around doing little for a half hour until you showed up and completed your work; the company just wasted money. If the company now has to pay those workers overtime to finish their work, who is management going to blame? You will be subject of management's scorn.

Another possibility is that management will expect the workers who were delayed by you to finish their work within the normal work day. There go those bathroom breaks again. Who do you think those workers will be angry at? Sure they will be angry a bit at management. But it is you being late that caused the tough work day, so it is you, their "bad workplace neighbor" who they will be annoyed with the most. You will be creating problems in the workplace, and if tardiness (even 5 minutes) is a repeat problem, you stand an excellent chance of being fired.

Your supervisor will have no choice. If you come late, others will expect management to deal with you or they will start coming late to work as well. That would throw off work schedules even more, increase costs through overtime, and mean missing customers' deadlines, which could result in losing those customers which mean lower profits. And by now you know that lower profits means fewer jobs and less money for employees. What a mess your five, ten or thirty-minute tardiness created.

Businesses can't risk it. Therefore, being tardy is a sure way to get fired.

Straight forward: reporting times for work are part of the company's policies making not reporting on time a serious offense with a consequence which is, almost assuredly, being fired.

ESOL EXERCISE WB3

Q1. What is the closest meaning for tardy?

    A. Unfriendly
    B. Unreliable
    C. Inconsistent
    D. Late

Q2. Unexcused absences are bad. Being tardy is bad. Please combine these two sentences into one sentence.

_____

_____

Q3. Using all your sick days, even when you are not really sick is bad. Using your sick days only when you are really sick is good. Please combine these two sentences into one sentence.

_____

_____

_____

_____

Q4. Using all your sick days, even when you are not really sick is bad. Please add details to this sentence from the information in the book by adding because and then listing one reason.

Using all your sick days, even when you are not really sick is bad because_____

_____

_____

Q5. Phrasal Verb is a combination of a verb and an adverb (or a verb and a preposition, or both), where the combination has a meaning different from the meaning of the words considered separately. Which sentence below uses a phrasal verb?

    A. I asked around, but no one knew the sick day policy.
    B. Jack Harkness knew the sick day policy.
    C. What is the sick day policy?
    D. The company allows five sick days a year.

Q5B. What words in you answer to Q5 is the phrasal verb?

_____

Q6. A verb is in the Passive Voice when the subject of the sentence is acted on by the verb. Which sentence below is written in passive voice?

    A. Sally Sparrow used three sick days last year.
    B. How many sick days did Sally Sparrow use last year?
    C. Sally Sparrow was sick yesterday.
    D. At work, Sally Sparrow missed three sick days last year.

*****

Phone center example

To show you how quickly a phone center can get out of control, let's say a co-worker of yours comes in 15 minutes late (I know you wouldn't come in late). During those 15 minutes callers are on hold longer than usual because the phone center is down one staff member, so 10 callers hang up because they have to leave to go to work. These 10 <u>dissatisfied</u> customers are now going to call back later in the day adding unexpected call volume to those time frames. Let's say that all ten call during their lunch break. Now the phone center is understaffed during lunch because it was staffed for ten less calls than it gets. So during lunch time callers will be on hold longer than expected and some of them will hang up because they have to eat. This creates more dissatisfied customers and adds more unexpected call volume to other time periods in that day or the next day. That in turn will create even more dissatisfied customers and create future time periods where there will be more calls, longer hold times than desired and additional customer hang-ups.

As you now see, this fifteen minute tardiness could result in a problem that lasts for days and causes many customers who are dissatisfied. And dissatisfied customers could take their business elsewhere reducing the profitability of the business. This, as we know, can have a negative impact on employee jobs, compensation, and benefits.

Now if you added in the fact some workers come back late from lunch, or take a bathroom break at a bad time, or call in with an unexcused absence, etc. you see the importance of being punctual and not taking off days unnecessarily.

Q1. You are a top employee working in a phone center. The company hires a new employee and much to your surprise it is a good friend of yours. This is someone you know will be a good employee but is also someone who constantly shows up late when meeting you places. You know you will have to give your friend advice about why that cannot happen here at work, especially in the phone center.

Wait until you are called on and then speak to the class (give advice) as if the class is your friend.

*****

Attendance and tardiness worksheet

1. What problems can arise from employees who are absent a lot and constantly tardy?

_____

_____

_____

_____

_____

_____

2. How does an employee benefit from good attendance and being punctual (on time)?

_____

_____

_____

_____

_____

3. What will you do to ensure you will get to work on time every day?

_____

_____

_____

_____

_____

_____

4. What are some of your personal lifestyle habits and obstacles that could hinder your efforts to get to work on time and be punctual while on the job?

_____

_____

_____

_____

_____

_____

5. List some contingency plans and strategies to help overcome the items you listed in #4 above.

_____

_____

_____

_____

_____

_____

EXERCISE WB2

Below is a list of reasons workers use for staying home from work. Please indicate if the excuse is good, bad, or depends upon the circumstance. Then explain why you believe the choice you made is the correct choice.

REASON	CIRCLE DECISION	EXPLAIN WHY
Q1. Your car will not start.	Good Bad Depends	
Q2. Your child is sick.	Good Bad Depends	
Q3. You stayed out late, are very tired, and wake up with a major headache.	Good Bad Depends	
Q4. You have a fever of 102.	Good Bad Depends	

Q5. You have an appointment with the local cable company scheduled that day.	Good Bad Depends	
Q6. There is a death in your family.	Good Bad Depends	
Q7. Your best friend needs to you watch his or her kids because they have a doctor's appointment.	Good Bad Depends	
Q8. You had a fight with your spouse and are too upset to work.	Good Bad Depends	
Q9. You have a second, part-time job and they told you, "We need you today three people are out with the flu; if you can't come in today and help out we will need to fire you and hire someone who can fill in when we have emergencies."	Good Bad Depends	
Q10. Your child's teacher called and needs to talk to you about something very important.	Good Bad Depends	

*****

ESOL Proper Absence and Tardiness Reporting Procedures Worksheet

Task #1: You are going to miss work because you are legitimately very sick.

How would you report this?

_____

_____

_____

When you would you report this?

_____

_____

_____

Who would you report this to? _____

Task #2: You find out today that you will need to take a day off for personal reasons in three weeks.

How would you request this?

_____
_____
_____

When you would you request this?

_____
_____
_____

Who would you ask for the day off? _____

Task #3: You are late getting back from lunch because of a car accident on the road. You find yourself stuck in traffic at the 5 minutes before the time you are supposed to be back from your lunch break. You know you will be about 20 minutes late getting back from work and your supervisor will not be happy because there is a busy day at work. What should you do?

_____
_____
_____
_____
_____

Task #4: Break out into groups and share the information you wrote down for this worksheet. Come to a group decision on the best answers for each situation (absence, future day off, tardiness).

Task #5: When called on present the group's decisions on the proper things to do for each situation (absence, future day off, tardiness). Everyone in the group needs to take part in the presentation.

Safety in the Workplace

For some reason the word safety always makes me think of an underrated song and album from the late seventies, "Safety in Numbers" by Crack the Sky. If you don't know it; check it out on You Tube. A little known fact is that their debut album, *Crack the Sky*, released in 1975, was declared the debut album of the year by *Rolling Stone* magazine and included memorable songs such as, "A Sea Epic" and "Robots for Ronnie." Oh, well, now on to the topic.

All workplaces have safety rules. Some rules are generated by the company, but most are required by OSHA (Occupational Safety and Health Administration). If companies do not follow these rules they can get fines or even shut down until proper safety precautions are implemented.

From the OSHA web site: "Under the OSH Act, employers are responsible for providing a safe and healthful workplace. OSHA's mission is to assure safe and healthful workplaces by setting and enforcing standards, and by providing training, outreach, education and assistance. Employers must comply with all applicable OSHA standards. Employers must also comply with the General Duty Clause of the OSH Act, which requires employers to keep their workplace free of serious recognized hazards."

OSHA enforcement information follows (from the OSHA web site):

OSHA Jurisdiction:

- Covers private sector employers
- Excludes self-employed, family farm workers, and government workers (except in state plan states)
- Approves and monitors 27 State Plan states which cover private and public sector employees.
- Assists Federal Agency Programs

OSHA Inspections:

- Conducted without advance notice
- On-site inspections, or Phone/Fax investigations
- Highly-trained compliance officers

Inspection Priorities:

- Imminent danger
- Catastrophes
- Worker complaints and referrals
- Targeted inspections - high injury/illness rates, severe violators
- Follow-up inspections

Therefore, you must follow the safety rules in your workplace and wear the proper and required safety clothing and equipment. Also, ensure that your co-workers do the same. Do not look the other way. The only way for you to be safe, is for everyone to act safely. The person who starts an electrical fire is not necessarily the only one who will get hurt.

Some items you need to be aware of include:

✓ Know workplace warning signs (physical signs or tags):
   - white/black = housekeeping hazards
   - green = first aid and safety equipment
   - blue = caution against using unsafe equipment
   - orange = physical hazards
   - red = danger, stop, and fire protection equipment
   - yellow = general caution

✓ Working with electricity
   - do not fix electrical problems yourself
   - do not use machines with red or yellow tags
   - report machines not working properly or with frayed cords
   - always plug in machines with the power button off

✓ Fire extinguishers
   - locate all fire extinguishers so you know where they are before you need them
   - read the labels to know what type of fires each fire extinguisher is to be used for; using the fire extinguisher on the wrong type of fire can make the problem worse
   - class A fire extinguishers are for wood, paper, cloth, trash plastics
   - class B fire extinguishers are for flammable liquids (gasoline, oil, grease, acetone)
   - class C fire extinguishers are for electrical
   - class D are for metals
   - water (H_2O) extinguishers are for class A fires only
   - carbon dioxide (CO_2) extinguishers are for class B and C
   - dry chemical (DC) can be for A,B,C or just B,C

✓ Emergency evacuation
   - know where the exits are
   - know the evacuation procedure

✓ Injuries
  - know and wear all required safety equipment to avoid injuries
  - know where the medical emergency kit is located
  - always use latex gloves where dealing with blood spills
  - for serious problems seek medical help

Below are some statistics from the U. S. Department of Labor's web site for 2006:

Number of deaths   5,703

  Transportation related   2,423
  Assaults/violent acts   754
  Equipment/object related   983
  Falls   809
  Harmful substance/work environment   525
  Fires/explosions   201

Percent of workers:

  Who get hurt/sick on the job   4.4%
  Who missed time from injuries/illness   1.3%

While the percentages may look low, this means that almost a half a million workers got hurt or sick on the job in 2006.

Another way to look at the numbers is that on average over 13,000 people got injured or sick on the job, and over 15 people died on the job, every day in 2006.

Consequences of accidents on businesses

The equation to determine the success of a business is simple:
Revenues – Expenses = Profits

Businesses need to be profitable to stay in business, keeping its workers employed.

Revenues are the monies that the business makes selling its products or services.

Expenses are monies that it costs the business to operate.

Expenses include employee costs, and insurance such as workman's comp.

Expenses can be fixed (such as mortgage on a building) or variable (such as the number of workers hired to complete a specific job or contract).

If a business isn't making profits, and can not raise its prices or increase its sales, it cuts expenses.

Fixed costs cannot be cut; variable costs can be cut.

Accidents are an expense to a business.

Accidents can carry fines, result in shut downs, and increase the amount of money the business must pay for workers (workman) compensation insurance. This increases expenses.
Another result of accidents in the workplace could be bad press leading to negative word of mouth for the company. That can lead to a reduction in customers, which obviously, has a negative impact on revenues.

Increases in expenses and/or reductions in revenues means that the business will need to cut expenses (and, yes, employees and employee salaries and benefits are on the table for cuts).

Therefore, co-workers who are not safety conscious (i.e. who do not play by the company's "safety rules"), or who fake injuries to collect workers compensation, may just cost you your job, or cause you to get a lower pay increase, or even see your compensation or benefits cut. Everything is connected. The extra business expenses from workplace accidents, higher insurance premiums, and loss of revenue from bad press have to be taken from somewhere.

This is why minimizing accidents on the job is a joint venture between the workers and the business. In addition to caring about its employees health and safety, and meeting OSHA standards; it is just good business for a company to provide a safe work environment while it makes sense for all workers to follow all safety rules, procedures and policies to remain safe, healthy and employed at a good wage.

So be sure you and your co-workers work safely and that no one takes advantage of worker compensation insurance.

Now the following points should make sense and be important to you:

(1) When an employee uses worker's comp fraudulently it is not just between that worker and the company; that worker is placing you and your co-workers' jobs, benefits, and wages in jeopardy. Remember, if one worker gets away with it, more will try.

(2) There are some situations where using your personal medical insurance instead of workman's comp to pay for your medical expenses may be the best choice as you work in partnership with your employer to ensure your health and the health of that business.

Safety consequences worksheet

If It Wasn't True It Would Be Funny, Inc. averages three employee accidents a week, in part because of some employees not following safety procedures, and in part because the company does not have sufficient safety policies in place.

List three consequences that could happen to the business.

1. _____
   _____

2. _____
   _____

3. _____
   _____

Assuming you worked for this company, list two consequences that could happen to you because of the situation at If It Wasn't True It Would Be Funny, Inc.

1. _____
   _____

2. _____
   _____

Steps to Take to Limit Accidents at Work

Be alert for possible dangers. Knowing the type of emergencies that may occur in your workplace means that you will be better prepared to avoid those dangers.

Keep your mind on your work. By concentrating on the work at hand there is a lower probability of an accident occurring.

Get training (formal or informal) on the proper and safe use of all equipment that you will be using in the workplace. The better you are trained, the less likely you will have an accident due to the lack of understanding of how to the use that equipment; and the more aware you will be regarding the potential dangers of using that equipment incorrectly.

Check your workplace for the location of safety equipment. If you know where equipment such as fire extinguishers, first aid kits, etc., are, you can respond to an accident more quickly and minimize the damage.

Know what to do if an accident occurs. By being prepared for common workplace accidents you can respond properly to emergency situations and avoid making the situation worse.

You are a full time employee for Electric Electricians located at 111 Main Street, Ridgway, PA. You are a tradesperson whose occupation is an electrician.

While on the job you sprain your wrist when you brace your fall off a ladder while doing electrical work in the ceiling while working at 222 First Street, DuBois, PA. It is not serious but will need to be wrapped for three weeks. First aid was administered at the work site and that was the only treatment needed. When you leave the area it is safe. The incident happened on January 25th, 2006 at 11:15 AM. The agency of the injury was powered equipment. You decide not to notify the Department of Industrial Relations.

The name of the W.H.S.O. is Bill Jones. His phone number is 555-111-2222.

The form that follows is used for all accidents at If It Wasn't True It Would Be Funny, Inc. Once completed, your supervisor will sign the form. There are no other attachments needed for this incident.

Use the form on the next page and fill it out using the information in Exercise WB3

Sample accident report

INCIDENT NOTIFICATION FORM

READ NOTES / DIRECTIONS PRIOR TO COMPLETION OF THIS FORM – PLEASE PRINT

Elect
Act 2

Work
and S
1995

Type of incident
☐ work injury ☐ serious bodily injury ☐ work caused illness ☐ dangerous event ☐ dangerous electrical event
Notify Department of Industrial Relations ☐ Yes ☐ No   ☐ serious electrical incident
Was injury/illness fatal? ☐ Yes ☐ No   If an electrical incident, has the area been made safe? ☐ Yes ☐ No

Details of injured person

Given names		Surname	
Residential Address		D.O.B.	
	Postcode	☐ Male ☐ Female	

Basis of employment

Full time	☐	Part time	☐
Casual	☐	Volunteer	☐
Member of public	☐	Other	☐
Self-employed	☐		

Type of employment

Occupation

Administration	☐	Tradesperson	☐	Apprentice/trainee	☐
Technical	☐	Professional	☐	Student	☐
Other	☐				

Nature of work injury or work caused illness, eg. fracture, sprain & strain, electrical shock, burns, etc.

Bodily location of injury or work caused illness

Medical treatment ☐ nil ☐ first aid ☐ doctor only ☐ hospital admitted to:
(if overnight)

Mechanism of injury/disease

Falls, trips and slips	☐	Sound and pressure	☐	Biological factors	☐
Hitting objects with part of body	☐	Body stressing	☐	Mental stress	☐
Heat radiation and electricity	☐	Chemicals and other substance	☐	Other and unspecified mechanisms of injury	☐

Agency of injury/disease

Machinery and (mainly) fixed plants	☐	Mobile plant and transport	☐	Animal, human and biological agencies	☐
Powered equipment, tools and appliances	☐	Non-powered handtools, appliances and equipment	☐	Environmental agencies	☐
Chemicals and chemical products	☐	Materials and substances	☐	Other and unspecified agencies	☐

Details of how incident occurred

Day   Month   Year   Time of incident: ☐ ☐ ☐ ☐ am/pm
Description of incident (Attach report)

Name of employer/self-employed person/principal contractor	
Address of employer/ self-employed person/ principal contractor	Location address of workplace where incident occurred
Name of W.H.S.O. and phone no. (if any)	Phone ( )

Employer/Self-Employed Person/Principal Contractor Signature

	Day	Month	Year

OFFICE USE ONLY	
District Reference No. ☐☐☐☐☐☐☐	Action
Plant No. ☐☐☐☐☐☐☐	
Date: Day Month Year	
Workplace/Construction Workplace No. ☐☐☐☐☐☐	
Licence No.	

PRIVACY STATEMENT The Department of Industrial Relations respects your privacy and is committed to protecting personal information. The information provided on this form is for

(Refer Reverse Page)

*****

The machines Fred works on give off sparks. Everyone is required to wear safety goggles (OSHA requirement). Fred's wife Wilma comes to the plant to give Fred his lunch box that he left at home. She is dressed in her work clothes for her job and walks directly up to Fred at his work station and hands him his lunch box, says a couple of words and then leaves.

Q1. If you were Wilma would you have done the same thing?

Q2. Why or why not?

*****

ESOL EXERCISE WB5 (continuation of WB4)

Q1. When called on, explain the purpose of using safety goggles in a machine shop.

_____
_____
_____
_____
_____
_____

Q2. OSHA has specific training requirements that businesses must follow to comply with health and safety laws. This includes training that must be provided to their employees. The following website lists the type of training that must be done →

http://trainingtoday.blr.com/employee-training-resources/OSHA-Training-Requirements

If you are in a computer lab, go to the website; if not the instructor will provide you with a handout.

Think about a job you would like to get (or a job you currently have). Look at the list on the website or handout and determine two specific areas where you are required to be trained. When called on, inform the class of the job you selected, the two types of training that you believe are required for that job, and why you selected those two training topics.

Topic   Why
1. _____   _____
                             _____
                             _____
                             _____
                             _____

2. _____   _____
                              _____
                              _____
                              _____
                              _____

Q3. Look at the list of "Some items you need to be aware of include:" (the items with the ✓). When called upon by the instructor, using the information referenced above, give advice (one specific item only) regarding safe behaviors in the workplace.

_____
_____
_____
_____
_____
_____

*****

ESOL EXERCISE WB6

What follows is information directly from OSHA Factsheet E1. Please read the information and then, working in groups assigned by the instructor, be prepared to make a presentation on what you read. For your group presentation, make an outline of what you plan to say. This means make a list of the topics you plan to talk about, with a short note to yourself next to the topic to remind you of the main thing you want to be sure to say for each topic (do not have full scripts or write-ups of what you are going to say, just the topics and short notes to yourself). When called on by the instructor, take turns with all group members participating in the presentation.

OSHA Factsheet E1 Information

There are many ways to reduce ergonomic risk factors and help fit the workplace to the worker. Solutions can be grouped into three main categories: eliminate the hazard, improve work policies and procedures, and provide personal protective equipment. Often the best solution involves a combination of approaches.

> **BEFORE YOU PROCEED** – here is the definition of ergonomic: intended to provide optimum comfort and to avoid stress or injury (especially of workplace design).

Eliminate the Hazard

The most effective way to control ergonomic hazards is to eliminate the risk factors altogether. Sometimes you can change the tools, equipment, job design, or work area to remove the hazard completely. This is called using "engineering controls."

These are some examples of engineering controls:

- Redesign workstations and work areas to eliminate reaching, bending, or other awkward postures.
- Provide adjustable tables and chairs that can be used by workers with a range of sizes and shapes, and that allow neutral postures.
- Provide carts for transporting material and mechanical hoists to eliminate lifting.
- Use tools that fit the hand, have no sharp edges, and eliminate awkward hand and wrist positions.
- Change where materials are stored to minimize reaching.
- Design containers with handles or cutouts for easy gripping.

Improving the workplace is the heart of ergonomics: changing the work to fit the worker. The design should accommodate the wide range of people assigned to the task.

Improve Work Policies and Procedures

The next most effective solution is to develop work policies, procedures, and practices that change how the job is done. This is called using "administratie controls."

These are some examples of administrative controls:
- Rotate workers among different tasks to rest the various muscle groups of the body, reduce repetition, and ease mental demands.
- Improve work scheduling to minimize excessive overtime or shift work which can cause fatigue.
- Increase staffing to reduce individual workloads.
- Provide sufficient breaks, since adequate recovery time can reduce fatigue.
- Assign more staff to lifts of heavy objects.
- Encourage proper body mechanics and use of safe lifting techniques (see box on next page).
- Require all loads to be labeled with their weight.
- Store heavy objects at waist height.
- Follow good housekeeping practices. Keep floors free of slipping or tripping hazards. Maintain power tools properly to reduce vibration. Keep cutting and drilling tools sharp to reduce the force required.
- Provide workers with training on safe working postures, lifting techniques, ergonomics policies and procedures, and the safe use of lifting and carrying devices.

Training is a critical element of nearly any solution and provides an important opportunity for worker participation. However, it is not a substitute for reducing risk factors and should be used in combination with engineering and administrative controls.

Safe Lifting Techniques

Lifting can put great strain on your back. Lifting from the floor can be particularly risky. For example, lifting a 25-pound box from the floor requires about 700 pounds of back muscle force, even when you bend your knees. Below are some tips that can help protect your back when you need to lift heavy objects.

- Try out the load first. If it is too bulky or heavy, get help.
- Avoid lifts that require stretching or bending to reach the load. Redesign the work area so objects you lift are close to the body and at waist height.
- Don't lift awkward objects such as long pipes or large boxes by yourself. Get help or use mechanical assists.
- When lifting, keep your back straight and lift with your legs.
- Lift slowly and carefully and don't jerk the load around.
- Keep the load as close to your body as possible while lifting it.
- Don't twist or turn your spine while carrying the load.
- Make sure your path is clear while carrying the object. Remove obstacles that could cause you to trip.

A program to teach workers how to lift properly should be used in combination with workplace redesign that reduces the amount of lifting needed. Remember, if materials are too heavy or awkward to lift and carry safely, get help, redesign the materials to be lighter and easier to handle, or use mechanical assists such as hoists, carts, or conveyors.

Provide Personal Protective Equipment

While more permanent solutions are being found and implemented, or if you are unable to redesign the job or equipment to eliminate risks, personal protective equipment (PPE) can be used.

PPE that can help address ergonomic problems includes:

- Knee pads for kneeling tasks.
- Shoulder pads to cushion loads carried on the shoulder.
- Gloves to protect against cold, vibration, or rough surfaces.

A CAUTION ABOUT BACK BELTS

Back belts are sometimes provided as PPE. Back belts have been studied extensively, and experts have concluded that they are not effective in preventing back injuries. Some believe that, in fact, they may cause injury by encouraging workers to lift heavier objects or by making muscles weaker. Most importantly, they do not make workers stronger or more able to perform a lift that is awkward or too heavy. The National Institute for Occupational Safety and Health (NIOSH) recommends that employers not rely on back belts to protect workers. Instead, it recommends that employers implement a comprehensive ergonomics program that includes workplace assessment, hazard reduction, and worker training.

Establish a Comprehensive Ergonomics Program

Employers should establish an ergonomics program to minimize musculoskeletal disorders. Elements of a good program include:

- Management commitment
- Worker involvement
- An organizational structure to get the work done, such as an ergonomics team or committee
- Training and education of workers and supervisors
- Job evaluation to identify risk factors
- Hazard prevention and reduction or elimination of risk factors
- Early detection and treatment of ergonomic injuries, and medical management of injury cases
- A system for workers and supervisors to report ergonomic problems, symptoms, and injuries without reprisal
- Ongoing evaluation of the ergonomics program.

OUTLINE (use as much or as little of the following table that you need to complete your outline)

TOPIC	NOTES

*****

The instructor will perform a search on OSHA safety signs and then a search on HAZMAT (hazardous materials) signs using Google and the image search and show the search results on the classroom computer projector. When called on choose one of the safety or HAZMAT signs and explain why it is an important sign that needs to be used to avoid work related hazards or accidents. If the instructor does not have a computer with projector and screen; then you will be provided with a handout.

OPTIONAL – work in groups assigned by the instructor and give a presentation on the importance of safety and HAZMAT signs. Include some specific examples of signs that the group giving the presentation need to be aware of because of their current or hoped-for jobs.

Be a Positive Force in the Workplace

The old children's show host, Mr. Rogers was right. "Be a good neighbor." Living next to someone who blasts loud music all the time, lets his/her lawn grow wildly, is the king (or queen) of the pop over, is constantly arguing very loudly, throws trash on the common grounds, doesn't pick up after his/her dog, allows his/her kids to play loudly outside at 7:00 ΛM Saturday morning, etc., is annoying. This neighbor is someone who doesn't know how (or chooses not) to be a good neighbor.

In life, you may have limited options to escape that self-centered neighbor. Work is different. Part of everyone's job is to be a good neighbor to other workers. If you are superb in your work, but are a "bad workplace neighbor", you may not get the pay raises you expect. You certainly are unlikely to get a promotion where you will be in charge of those neighbor workers. You could even get fired.

Think about it. Your employer needs more than one good worker. So, even if you are the best worker but your "bad workplace neighbor" actions result in other workers being unhappy at work, who can the company afford to lose; you or three or four others? Furthermore, if other workers were to leave because of a bad work environment due to a "bad workplace neighbor" it is usually good workers who leave because they will be the most **coveted** by other employers.

Therefore, it is very difficult for a business to keep a good worker who is a "bad workplace neighbor." Worst case, the supervisor gives that employee a mixed performance appraisal (usually this comes with only a below-average to average pay raise). The supervisor's hope is that that employee will improve as a workplace neighbor to get a larger raise during his/her next performance review.

So while many workers believe their pay is only about doing their job well, that is not true. Their supervisor cannot overlook bad behavior in the workplace. High employee turnover (workers constantly leaving) is very expensive, cutting into business profits (and we now know that can negatively impact jobs and wages). New employees have to be trained; meaning that a person in the company is training a new employee rather than being productive elsewhere. Also, new employees need time before they are at full productivity (takes time before the new employee can produce work at expected levels) so it costs the company more money to produce the same amount of work until the new employee is up to speed.

Even if workers' "bad workplace neighbor" behaviors do not cause their fellow employees to quit, it will still have a negative impact on overall productivity. Workers who are unhappy in the workplace often make more mistakes, look for any excuse to be absent from work, and think about their job as short term, not long term, so come up with fewer suggestions to solve customer and work related problems.

Luckily for the employer, if these problems can be solved by firing one employee, even if he/she is a top employee in terms of productivity and quality of work, it can, and often will, do so.

Entering the workplace is like moving to a foreign country. Some of the behaviors needed to be a good neighbor in the country will be common sense, while others have to be explained and, possibly, learned.

ESOL EXERCISE WB8

Q1. What is the meaning of the word coveted, printed in bold on the previous page?

    A. hated
    B. trusted
    C. ignored
    D. desired

Q2. Which statement is TRUE:

    A. If you are very good on the job, your employer will love you and you will get big pay raises even if you are a problem in the workplace.
    B. If you're a problem in the workplace, that's okay as long as you are very good at your job.
    C. Being a "good neighbor" to both your co-workers and your supervisors is part of your job.
    D. If you do not perform your work very well, but are a "good neighbor" to your co-workers and your supervisors you will be considered a top employee who will get big pay raises.

*****

What follows are some common behaviors workers will need to follow to become "good workplace neighbors." I'm sure many of you will find the majority of these as common sense; behaviors you would do in the workplace even if you hadn't read this book. That's fine. But the one or two that you may not have known will help you, and now you know that the items that follow below are expected in the workplace, not optional if you want to keep your job and maximize your pay.

Be dependable and responsible

Dependable refers to the person, while responsible refers to a person's action. It is a fact that you must show up to work when scheduled and never be late. I'm confident that you will, as the famous Starship Captain Picard says, "Make it so." By performing this one feat you attain a workplace behavior highly-valued by employers; being dependable. Your supervisor will know he/she can count on you being at work when he/she needs you at work. This will help you keep your job. But is it enough? No, it is not. If your employer can depend on you, but cannot rely on you to get your job done, then your dependability will go somewhat unnoticed.

However, if you are responsible by completing all your work assignments satisfactorily, and combine that with being dependable, you become a highly-valued employee, and will be on your way to a long successful working career.

Grooming

Everyone knew that guy or gal in college who partied all night, came home very late and kept hitting the snooze button on his/her alarm clock until he/she finally got up five minutes before class was starting. Still reeking badly from the odors of his/her night on the town, but with no time to shower, he/she runs off to class au natural (makes me think of the old theme song from the television show *The Monkees*, "Here we come, walking down the street, get the funniest looks from everyone we meet"). Or worse, he/she takes a "deodorant shower" (or the just as bad "laying on the perfume/after shave shower" mixing bad smells with over-powering factory-created smells). It didn't work then and doesn't work now. While in college that may have been overlooked because of the "hey I might need to do that some day" factor; in the workplace it will not. Co-workers will avoid working next to that person at all costs and may complain to supervisors. Depending upon the supervisor's personality, he/she will either confront the "smelly worker," will give the co-worker assignments where he/she is working alone, or will do nothing. It is the second and third options that will doom the "smelly worker." In the case of separating that worker from the other workers in the "pack," that worker's future with the company is dead in the water. In the case where the situation is ignored, the smelly worker's days with the company could be numbered.

So do not party all night, roll out of bed and come to work. If you do you are just shooting yourself in the foot by being a "bad workplace neighbor."

The second topic in this section is a bit more delicate. Most of you reading this will think, "Duh, why even mention it?" However, you may have known someone in your life who did not follow what is written next. Some may be individuals who came to the United States from overseas where daily practices are different. Below are standard hygiene practices used in the United States and will need to be followed to be considered a "good workplace neighbor."

- ✓ Shower every day using soap
- ✓ Use deodorant every day before coming to work
- ✓ Brush your teeth every day before coming to work
- ✓ Use mouthwash every morning
- ✓ Make sure your hair is neat and clean every day
- ✓ Wear clean and odor free clothes to work every day
- ✓ Wear clothes that are appropriate for your workplace
- ✓ Do not use too much perfume/cologne/after shave, (many people are sensitive to smell)

When called on, inform your instructor of the job you would like realistically like to have (it can be your current job or a different job than your current job).

Task #1: Write down the job that each student mentions in the chart below along with how you believe that person should dress for the workplace for that job.

For your next class session, come to class dressed as you would for the job that you mentioned in class. When called on remind the class of your job and explain why you chose the clothing you are wearing.   The instructor will inform you if that is correct or if there is something you can do to improve your clothing for the workplace for your job.

Task #2: Compare what you wrote down for each job with the correct clothing for that job.

NAME	JOB	PROPER CLOTHING	CORRECT yes or no

Mannerisms and habits

Since there are a lot of people with diverse behaviors that comprise a workplace; rules are established to avoid workplace conflicts. Many of these rules get in the way of individuals habits. However, think of this like a clubhouse, gym, pool, tennis court, etc. in your community. There are all sorts of rules governing these shared places. For example, no running by the pool (slip and fall in a wet area, have an accident, the accident costs the community pool money, insurance rates increase, and suddenly it costs every member of the community more money to use the pool – just like a safety issue in business).

Therefore, to be a "good workplace neighbor" and a valuable employee, play by the rules of the workplace as it relates to personal behavior. If smoking is not allowed in the workplace, don't smoke. If there is a designated smoking area and you are a smoker, use it. If you are not allowed to eat at your desk, don't sneak food at your desk.

Also, be very conscious of your own bad habits and mannerisms. Your mom will look the other way and still love you if you use profanity (but probably be hiding a dirty look), but your co-workers and supervisor will not. For many people, using profanity is something that they do without thinking. It is not, however, something you should do at work. Even if you are not called on it, using profanity in your everyday speech or when angry at work will be viewed as unprofessional and limit your growth in the company. In fact, the supervisor that tells you to stop is doing you a favor because he/she is giving you an opportunity to correct that bad habit at work. The supervisor that says nothing has probably already limited your growth to your current job position in his/her mind. It is almost never that the supervisor thinks it is okay that you use profanity because even if he/she is not offended, he/she knows someone in the workplace will be, and will have options available to him/her to get the profanities to stop which will make the supervisor look bad.

There are other mannerisms and habits that people have that they can use with the people that know them well, but are inappropriate in the workplace. Examples include touching people on the shoulder when talking to them, giggling, chewing gum, telling ethnic-related jokes, etc. I cannot list them all. If you do not know yours, ask someone that knows you and do not be offended when you hear what that person tells you.

Grooming and bad habit worksheet

Look at the previous pages with the list of grooming items and bad mannerisms and habits.

Which grooming items do you need to add to you routine to comply with what is expected at work?

_____   _____   _____

What bad mannerisms and habits do you need to correct in order to comply with what is expected at work?

1. _____

2. _____

What habits do you currently have that you know you will have to curtail to assure that you are a "good workplace neighbor?"

1. _____

2. _____

3. _____

Positive attitude

Everyone likes to be around people with positive attitudes. It's infectious. At work, it is more than that. Workers who look at things in a negative light and communicate that negativity to other workers (either verbally or with negative nonverbal personal signals) are considered problems in the workplace by management.

If every time a supervisor informs his/her team of new work procedures, you say nothing but sit there with your arms crossed and a frown, you will be labeled a malcontent without even opening up your mouth!

Therefore, I have two pieces of advice depending upon your personality.

If you are someone who looks at the glass as half empty, someone who always initially reacts poorly to change, do not discuss your feelings with your co-workers. You will come across as negative and that will be a very big problem for you. Also, when you are being informed of changes make an effort win an academy award. That doesn't mean over act, but be conscious of your body language and avoid negative personal signals. The gloom and doom co-worker is a horrible "workplace neighbor."

On the other hand, if you are someone who looks at the glass as half full, someone who initially reacts positively to change, and tends to become a cheerleader for the cause, let your positive attitude shine through. Your co-workers will appreciate it since they will have to adapt to the changes and seeing that someone feels positive about the changes will make them feel good. Even better, your supervisor will appreciate your attitude and consider you a real team player.

Positive self-image

The previous topics were to help you be a "good workplace neighbor" in your interactions with others. This topic is to help put you in the right frame of mind to undertake that challenge.

Always remember that you are working in your job because the management of the company believed in you enough to hire you. The company's profits are based on the quality of work received from its employees, including you, so that was a big decision.

The company believes in you, the management of the company believes in you, so you should believe in yourself. Have a positive self-image!

Know that you were chosen for your job. That despite any negative vibes you may feel are going on around you, and despite some occasional negative comments being communicated to you, that you are still employed so management still believes in you. If your supervisor did not believe in you, you would have been fired. That doesn't mean your supervisor believes you are working at your peak performance levels. He/she may believe that there is room for improvement. However, in the end he/she believes you are contributing to the profitability of the business, that you are not just a drain on the company's expenses. Again, if you were, you would be fired.

So feel good about your role in the company and be a "good workplace neighbor." Also know that your supervisor is on your side. As in sports, some coaches (supervisors) are players-coaches (think Tony Dungy), while some coaches can be tough SOB's on their players (think Bill Parcells). In both cases, however, the coach (supervisor) wants, in fact, needs his players to play well. Their jobs are on the line. Even when genius coaches don't win enough, they get fired. So despite how tough your supervisor is on you, know that he/she wants, in fact, needs you to succeed.

Next, a positive self-image does not mean you must be perfect all the time. Even the great ones make mistakes. In a game in 2007, Hall of Fame coach, Joe Gibbs used back-to-back timeouts to freeze a field goal kicker. That was against the rules, something he should have known. He made a mistake. The result was a penalty on his team, making the kick a much easier one and his team lost because of that made field goal. You will make mistakes as well. The key is to learn from those mistakes and to not repeat the same ones. Also, to ask questions if you are unsure of something. Just take notes so you do not have to keep asking the same question over and over again.

Lifestyle compromises

If you were playing in a championship game tomorrow, you wouldn't spend the night before the game partying and drinking into the wee hours of the morning. At least you wouldn't if you wanted to be at your best for the game. Now if you win the game, celebrating could be in order the night after the game.

At work, everyday is like a championship game. If you don't do your job to the best of your ability, your business could lose customers. If your productivity is down you are not producing sufficient product, meeting customer time schedules, etc., etc., etc. In the end that means less profits for the business which means less job security and less money available for employee salaries. It also means that your job performance is below standard, your supervisor will notice that, and that could result in lower pay raises and less opportunities for advancement. It could also result in you being fired.

Therefore, if you like to go out and "party", do so on a night where you do not have work the next day. This will ensure that you can report to work on time, and that there will be no lasting effects from the prior night negatively impacting your work.

Another compromise you may have to make because of your "marriage-like" relationship with your employer is your bed time. To be at your best you need a good night's sleep. Be sure you get it. Today, with DVR, DVD recorders, TiVo, shows available on the Internet, etc., you can easily watch any late night show you like another time.

You also need to be aware that how you behave outside of work reflects on your employer. How many times have you met an obnoxious person, found out where he/she works and thought that's one place I'll never go to. So do not do anything that could drive customers away from your place of business (that includes making negative comments about the company you work for). The impact on you can only be negative, even if the behaviors and/or comments never get traced back to you. If your place of work suffers, it just leads to layoffs and less money available for you and your co-workers.

This also means be careful what you post on YouTube and Facebook. You are a representative of your company. Be sure you behave accordingly online as well as in your everyday life.

Lifestyle choices

There are things you can do in your everyday life to help you be the best you can be in your partnership with your employer. Many these will also help you outside of the workplace as well.

- ✓ Eat healthy
- ✓ Exercise
- ✓ Don't overindulge in alcohol
- ✓ Don't use illegal drugs
- ✓ Don't smoke

Take control of your life

One of the best ways to take control of your life is to hang out with friends who understand that you are serious about earning good money in the workplace, support you in your quest, and are positive influences in your quest. These are not people who get down on you because you no longer go out partying with them on Wednesday nights. These are people who understand your priorities and start getting together with you Friday nights (assuming you have off Saturdays and Sundays) instead.

Know that you are in control of what you do, and what you do not do. Take control of your life and do not just follow others. Know that things happen for a reason and develop a plan so that good things happen for you. Decide on a plan of action in life, and at work, and follow that plan. Do not allow others to talk you out of what you know you have to do to succeed. This is especially true when things are not going the way you want. Stay the course. Know that "true friends" will not use this occasion to tear down your plan. True friends will be supportive. They may even help you come up with ways to adjust your plan so that you have a better chance to succeed. They will not substitute their selfish goals for you (e.g. as a buddy to party with when you're in a weak moment), for what is truly important to you (helping you stay the course so you can succeed at work).

Two examples of taking control through planning

One of your goals in life is to be a good employee so you can stay employed and earn good money. How do I know this? You wouldn't be reading this book or taking a work readiness course if it weren't true!

Therefore, both of these examples will deal with planning to get to work on time.

(1) To get to work on time, you need reliable transportation. Therefore you need to:
- ✓ Keep your car in good working order (repairs and maintenance).
- ✓ Know all public transportation options that can be used in case of emergencies (method and time schedules).
- ✓ Exchange telephone numbers with at least one co-worker who lives in your area so you can contact each other in case either of you need a ride to work (also know how early you need to call your co-worker to ensure that both of you do not arrive late to work).
- ✓ Ask your neighbors where they work. Some may work close to you and you both can give each other rides to work in emergencies.
- ✓ Know that, worst case, you can always call a cab to get to work; then let your supervisor know that you took a cab and ask if he/she knows anyone outside of your department that lives in your area and can help you out for the next day or two while your car is being repaired.

(2) If you have children, to be able to get to work on time (or at all), you need reliable daycare. Therefore you need to:
- ✓ Have both a reliable primary and backup daycare plan in place for your children (whether a facility or a worker in your home).
- ✓ Know the schedules of family members and friends you trust to take care of your children so they can be used in emergencies.
- ✓ Develop a network of neighborhood parents who have daycare needs and use each other's daycare workers in emergencies.
- ✓ Know your child's school schedule in advance so you will know when exceptions to your normal daycare plan will occur. This will protect against last minute hunting for daycare services; you will be able to plan in advance.

✓ Know all after school programs that can be of use to you. Also, know in advance days that the after school program may not be available even though the school is open so you can plan for those days.

✓ Investigate all daycare businesses or individuals that you plan to use. Be sure that they are dependable and that they offer safe environments for your children. Ask for references. If possible, show up at the facility before you plan to use them and ask the parents dropping off their kids questions. One good question to ask is how long they have been using the facility. If all are relatively new to the facility (and the facility has been around for years), that could mean that others have left because of previous problems. For businesses you can also contact the Better Business Bureau to see if there have been complaints about that business.

In both of these cases, if you do not get to work on time (or at all), your supervisor will not accept either car trouble or child care issues as acceptable reasons for missing work. Potential car trouble and child care issues are problems that people know may occur. You will be expected to have backup plans in place.

What it all means

"Married to the job" is a phrase usually reserved for workaholics. However, it is really true for everyone. Like a marriage there are benefits, responsibilities, and compromises required of both the employer and the employees.

The benefits are money, heath insurance, etc. for the employee, and quality work being completed for the employer.

The responsibilities are many for the employee, as outlined in this book. The responsibilities for the employer are to provide a safe, harassment-free, discrimination-free work environment and more to its employees.

Now it's the compromises that are interesting and are often ignored by employees. Employers compromise by giving up a greater share of profits than they would like to pay for their employees' salaries and benefits. The compromises required by employees involve their lifestyles away from the job.

When in a committed personal relationship, both parties have to make changes in their lifestyles. For example, going to single bars may no longer be acceptable. Well, since your relationship with your employer is like a marriage there are compromises you have to make in your lifestyle so you can be at your best for you employer.

Life plan for succeeding at work worksheet

Review the subchapters starting with lifestyle compromises through what it all means. List two things you will need to change, modify or have under control to ensure that you are successful at work.

1. _____

_____

2. _____

_____

Now list the steps you will take to ensure that the change is successful.

1. _____

_____

2. _____

_____

3. _____

_____

EXERCISE WB5

Q1. How can dependable employee be unreliable?

_____

_____

_____

Q2. How can a reliable employee be undependable?

_____

_____

_____

Q3. Which is more important, being dependable or being reliable?

_____

_____

_____

_____

Q4. You work as a fact checker and need to be alert on the job so that errors do not occur. You stay up late every night because you have a second job and often come to work very tired. You need the extra money. If your work suffers, will management understand and look the other way?   Yes   No   Maybe

What could be the consequence of working that second job?

_____

_____

_____

Q5. You show up late for work because you had to bail your best friend out of jail. You call to ask your new supervisor for permission and you get permission. Is that the end of it?
Yes   No   Maybe

Could anything negative come out of this situation for you?

_____

_____

_____

*****

ESOL EXERCISE WB9

Using the information **from** **this** **chapter** **only**, answer the following questions:

Q1. Write down the first step for the second example for taking control through planning

_____

_____

Q2. Write down the last step for the first example for taking control through planning

_____

_____

Q3. Locate the third step in the first example for taking control through planning. Write down the next step after the step you just located.

_____

_____

Q4. Locate the section heading "What it all means." Identify the linking words in the first paragraph of that section. Linking words help you to connect ideas and sentences, so that people can follow your ideas.

_____

Q5. What are three lifestyle choices that can help you be the best you can be:

_____

_____

_____

Q6. According to the information in this book, you should always remember that you are working in your job because

_____

_____

*****

Using the information **in** **this** **chapter** **only**; determine the three most important behaviors that you believe will help you succeed in the workplace. When called on by the instructor, inform the class of the three behaviors you selected and tell the class why you chose those three items.

1. _____

2. _____

3. _____

*****

Avoiding Workplace Problems

Who knew that the band The Offspring sung songs about the workplace! I have heard that when the band first formed they welcomed Kevin "Noodles" Wasserman, the school janitor into the band, allegedly because he was old enough to purchase alcohol for Dexter Holland and Greg Kriesel, both of whom were under the legal drinking age. So while their song, "She's Got Issues", contains the line, "And check your baggage at the door", the band didn't follow its own advice, bringing alcohol to their workplace. Wasserman acted unethically helping underage kids get alcohol (consequences - if one of them got into a car accident while drunk, killed someone, and it was found out that he supplied the alcohol, he could have been charged along with the driver). Oh, to be young, reckless, and in a successful rock band.

Their message, however, is on the money for the workplace. Check your baggage (behaviors that others will find objectionable) at the door of your workplace. This is not a suggestion. It is required. If you do not, you will likely be fired.

ESOL EXERCISE WB11

Q1. "Check your baggage at the door" is an idiom. What is the definition of an idiom.

    A. A word or phrase that you must take literally (precisely)
    B. A word or phrase that is not taken literally (precisely)
    C. A word or phrase that is meant to mean absolutely nothing
    D. A word or phrase that always refers to lyrics in a song

Q2. What makes "check your baggage at the door" an idiom.

_____

_____

_____

*****

Value of Diversity in the Workplace

Since the workplace is based on teamwork, the more diversified the team members, the stronger the team.

If a team has team members who can look at a challenge from a variety of backgrounds and viewpoints, the team stands a better chance of coming up with solutions that address all aspects of that challenge.

This includes a mix of workers of different gender, age, ethnicity, race, religion, etc. The company wants to do business with all customers. If a team is assembled to fix a problem, it is best if the people working on the solution can fairly represent the company's customers.

For that reason, companies that employ a large staff, often have a goal of assembling a diversified workforce. Many ill-advised workers may feel the diversification is due to pressure from forces outside the company. That is a foolish viewpoint. Workplace diversification is strength for a business.

Objectionable behaviors

What follows are behaviors that will get you fired on the spot. Be aware that is <u>not</u> <u>you</u> who decide if your behavior qualifies as one of these objectionable behaviors. It is a combination of the company and the person who finds the behavior objectionable. That is very important. I'll "say" it again, with emphasis this time. It is **not you** who determines if your behavior qualifies as one of these objectionable behaviors. It is a combination of the company and **the person who finds the behavior objectionable**.

Harassment

When most people think of harassment in the workplace, sexual harassment is the topic that comes to mind. However, harassment can also be racial, creed (religion), age, ethnicity, lifestyle, and handicap motivated.

Remember, it is not what you think is objectionable that defines your actions as harassment; it is company policies and what the object of the harassment thinks. A joke you tell innocently every day to your friends, with no malice intended, could be taken as harassment in the workplace.

Harassment can be in the form of words or actions. To help avoid harassment you need <u>to</u> <u>avoid</u>:

- ✓ Telling/distributing jokes making fun of specific groups of people
- ✓ Touching other people
- ✓ Commenting on a person's physical appearance (good or bad)
- ✓ Using words to describe groups of people that the group finds objectionable (slurs, slang, etc.)
- ✓ Making broad comments about groups of people (good or bad)
- ✓ Displaying photos, images, cartoons, etc. that contains materials, symbols, words, etc. that others find objectionable in your work area
- ✓ Cursing

Discrimination

The workplace, like our country, is a melting pot. You will interact with people of different races, creeds, ethnicities, lifestyles, and ages. You must treat <u>everyone</u> in your workplace with courtesy and respect. Who you hang out with, who you deal with in your personal life is up to you. Who you deal with, who you interact with in the workplace is up to your management. If you are organizing a company event, everyone must be allowed to attend. You cannot discriminate against the people in your workplace. If you do, the company will have to fire you.

Drug/alcohol abuse

You may drink or use recreational drugs in your personal life. However, if you come to work drunk, hung over, or high, you are seriously risking your job.

Using recreation drugs is illegal, hence unethical. With unethical behavior come potential consequences. In this case, the consequences will be you losing your job. Many places of employment have drug testing and make their employees sign a drug-free workplace pledge as a condition of employment. Using drugs is a serious workplace offense. It has brought down more than one professional athlete.

The same is true for alcohol. When you sign a drug-free workplace pledge, it includes alcohol. You cannot drink on the job, no matter how well you believe you can hold your liquor, and cannot show up drunk or hung over.

Violence

Violence in the workplace is not tolerated, even if no one is seriously hurt. If you have a temper, you must keep it in check. Just threatening violence could get you fired. If a co-worker gets you angry, just walk away.

A plan of action

There are attitudes you can adapt in the workplace to help you avoid missteps. They include:

1. Remember the Otis Redding written, Aretha Franklin made famous song, "Respect." Treat everyone with respect, the same respect with which you want to be treated.
2. Know that you are not in control; your management is in control. Be a good soldier.
3. Be color, gender, lifestyle, etc. blind.
4. When talking to others in the workplace, talk as is if everyone you know and care about is listening in (parents, kids, friends, neighbors, etc.).
5. When talking to others in the workplace, talk as if your supervisor is always watching, and your next pay raise is on the line.
6. Do not say anything about another person that you wouldn't want said about you.

7. In a heated argument, talk as though you are in a public library (talk softly, do not raise your voice) and that the local police and "ambulance-chasing" attorneys are present.
8. When interacting with others in friendly conversations keep your hands at your side (no touching).
9. Act as though your personal work space will be shown on the *Disney Channel* (everything rated "G").

Don't count on others in the workplace to follow this advice; if they do be pleasantly surprised. If they do not, walk away.

Workplace comportment worksheet

Indicate if each of the items in the previous checklist comes naturally for you (yes if it does, no if it does not).

1. Yes	No	2. Yes	No	3. Yes	No
4. Yes	No	5. Yes	No	6. Yes	No
7. Yes	No	8. Yes	No	9. Yes	No

EXERCISE WB6

Foad works for Tony at a bank. Tony is very big on team building and starts a monthly group get together after work on the last Friday night of the month at the local pub. Foad's religious beliefs prohibit drinking alcohol and eating certain foods.

If Tony did not know Foad's religious beliefs, what might his reaction be if:

Q1. Foad refused to join the group

_____
_____
_____
_____

Q2. Foad joined the group but refused to drink

_____
_____
_____
_____

Q3. Foad joined the group but refused to chip in for appetizers ordered by the group

_____
_____
_____
_____

Q4. If any of the above situations occurred, what problems could this have caused Foad at work?

_____
_____
_____
_____

Q5. If Tony knew about Foad's religious beliefs, how might he have reacted to ensure Foad's behavior was not a problem for him with his co-workers?

_____
_____
_____
_____

Q6. If Tony knew Foad's religious beliefs and still wanted to get his group together, what could he do differently?

_____
_____
_____
_____

*****

ESOL EXERCISE WB12

Q1. You find yourself in a situation where there is an employee harassing you (for the purposes of this exercise the person's name is Rickles). It is not direct to you; Rickles is making jokes about people who had to take ESOL courses to learn to speak English. Rickles also hangs cartoons that make fun of ESOL students and tells everyone he or she can that ESOL students make terrible employees.

Write a two paragraph note to your supervisor complaining about this situation.

_____
_____
_____
_____
_____
_____
_____
_____
_____
_____
_____
_____

_____

_____

_____

_____

_____

_____

_____

_____

_____

_____

_____

_____

_____

_____

_____

_____

_____

_____

Q2. What statement is true regarding a plan of action?

A. Something you should think about, formalize and start using to help you be successful.
B. Something that does not need to be thought about and implemented until a need arises.
C. Something that is required only by people in power (instructors, supervisors, etc.), but not something that you will need until you are in a position of power.
D. Something that only works in theory and is not practical for real life.

Q3. Based on the words in the sentences that follow, place them in order from the most likely to occur (the highest probability) to the least likely to occur (the lowest probability). Use 1 for most likely to occur based on the words; and 8 for least likely to occur based on the words.

STATEMENT	RANK 1 to 8
If I use any of the objectionable behaviors listed in this chapter , I'll possibly be fired	
If I use any of the objectionable behaviors listed in this chapter I'll definitely be fired.	
If I use any of the objectionable behaviors listed in this chapter, I probably won't be fired.	
If I use any of the objectionable behaviors listed in this chapter, I definitely won't be fired.	
If I use any of the objectionable behaviors listed in this chapter, I'll almost certainly be fired.	
If I use any of the objectionable behaviors listed in this chapter , I might not be fired.	
If I use any of the objectionable behaviors listed in this chapter, I'll likely be fired.	
If I use any of the objectionable behaviors listed in this chapter, I almost certainly won't be fired.	

*****

Social Life at Work

Have you ever heard the phrase, "don't mix business with pleasure?" Well, your business is your job, and your job takes place at work. Therefore, the social connections you make at work must be treated with even more care than those you make outside of the workplace. If you have a fight with a friend you do not work with, you do not have to see, or deal with that person unless you want to. That is not true for friendships you develop at work. Let's say a friend from your workplace violates your trust in a situation that has nothing to do with work, and that violation of trust happens away from the workplace. In other words, this violation of trust is of no interest and no consequence to the management of your company. However, you will still have to see and interact with that person. In fact, you may have to <u>rely on</u> this person at work. How well you do your job may be dependent on him/her, meaning that this person may have an impact on your next pay raise. Now you are in a bind. If you bring your personal conflict with this person to the workplace (not leaving your baggage at the door), then it <u>does</u> become of interest to management, and not in a good way. Management may feel that it has to let one of you go. Or, management may have to change someone's job functions (50% chance it's you). And it won't be a **step up**. If this personal issue moves to the workplace, it will be held against you, even if your supervisor says it won't (he/she may even believe that, but more senior management will not look at you as supervisor material if you cannot control your personal issues at work).

The answer is not to avoid making friends at work. I have many friends who I met at work throughout my career. My best friends at work, however, were not the people I sat next to, or whose work I needed to rely on. Those people I treated as **"friendly- neighbors."** These were people who I knew I might have to sit next to, or rely on at work, for a long time. These were people I could not afford to get into non-work related arguments with. So going to lunch with them yes; hanging out on Sunday watching football games, no. At times, after one of my "friendly-neighbor" co-workers moved on to another job, or when I moved on to another job, my friendship with some of my "friendly-neighbor" co-workers grew.

ESOL EXERCISE WB13

Q1. What is the meaning of "step up" (in bold) in the first paragraph?

    A. A fun job
    B. A job at a higher level in the company
    C. An important job
    D. A job with the company for which you are currently working

Q2. Which behavior below would you not do with a "friendly-neighbor" (in bold) as the term is used in the second paragraph of this chapter?

   A. Go to lunch
   B. Talk about your personal problems
   C. Ask for help with a work issue
   D. All of the three behaviors mentioned above are fine to do

Q3. An Adverb Clause is a group of words that is used to change or qualify the meaning of an adjective, verb, clause, adverb, or any other type of word or phrase (with the exception of determiners and adjectives that directly modify nouns). Which sentence below uses an adverbial clause?

   A. So in order to perform well at work, treat your co-workers as "friendly-neighbors."
   B. Treat your co-workers as "friendly-neighbors."
   C. What are "friendly-neighbors?"
   D. All of the three sentences above contain an adverbial clause.

*****

And if workplace friendships are this complicated, how complicated do you think office romances get?

Dating in the workplace

Employers expect their employees to "leave their issues at the door." When those issues involve an argument between co-workers who are dating, that is often difficult to do. In fact, co-workers dating can be so disruptive, that some businesses have a no dating a co-worker policy. Since not following company policies is unethical, if you decide to date a co-worker anyway, you can face severe consequences. One or both of you could be fired for violating company rules.

But what guidelines should you use if there is no company policy against dating in your workplace to avoid setbacks in your career and pay?

(1) Do not date someone who you work next to or whose work you rely on. Since dating comes with both good times and arguments, it will be almost impossible to avoid bringing your arguments to work if your dating partner is "in your face" all day at work. Besides, dating either leads to a permanent partnership or a breakup, with many more ending in a breakup than permanent partnership. More often than not, breakups are ugly, and people move on with their lives with the person he/she was previously dating no longer in his/her life. Obviously, that will not be the case if you dated a person you work with. Therefore, dating someone in this situation usually leads to one or both leaving a job that he/she was growing in, and starting over again in a new company. This can damage your resume, stunt your career growth, and put a dent in your earnings. Even if you stay with the company, the friction in the workplace can lead to your supervisor thinking you used poor judgment, and poor judgment is not a

characteristic valued by employers. And employees who are believed to have poor judgment are not employees who are viewed as management material.

Now, you may feel this is unfair. That if you do your job well, you personal life (dating) is not fair to be used against you by the company. Normally that is true. However, it was you that opened the door for your personal life (dating) to be an issue on the job by dating a co-worker you deal with on a regular basis and, therefore, making it impossible for you to "leave your issues at the door." When you cannot "leave your issues at the door" it becomes a workplace issue. In this case, even if you have the ability to separate work from personal life, the person you are/were dating may not be able to do that. He/she has the ability to bring *your* personal business into the workplace and you can do absolutely nothing about it.

(2) <u>If you decide to date someone in your workplace who does not work in your area, and whose work you do not rely on, make sure it is someone you truly believe has the potential to be a lifetime partner.</u> There are a lot of successful marriages that started with the people meeting in the workplace. Many, however, took time to develop. The individuals involved got to know each other very well at work, sometimes as friends, before they started dating. In fact, by the time they started dating, there was already a strong connection.

(3) <u>Workplace "Romeos" may be popular with his/her co-workers, but he/she is not looked at favorably by management.</u> In fact he/she is looked at as a potential source of workplace turmoil. As individuals feel used, or "get dumped" they begin to feel uncomfortable at work, and that has a negative impact on productivity and quality. So do not look at your workplace as your pool for casual dating. If you use your co-workers for "one-night stands" (even if your co-worker is a willing participant), don't be surprised if your employer treats you the same way and you're cut loose in a hurry.

(4) <u>Be very aware of the line between asking a co-worker on a date and sexual harassment.</u> If you ask someone on a date whose pay and/or performance appraisal you control, just the act of asking that person out is sexual harassment. That is true, even if the person says yes. That is because the root of sexual harassment is control and power, not sexual deviance. No worker should be concerned, even a little, that not accepting a date with someone at work could lead to a lower pay raise or an unwarranted bad performance evaluation. A person that controls a worker's pay raises and/or job evaluations has that power. Therefore he/she should <u>never</u> place another person in this position, even if he/she is doing so with good intentions, and would never use a decline to give that co-worker a low pay raise or bad performance appraisal.

This should be common sense, because it is not only the person being asked out that is being put in a bad position, but so is the person doing the asking. What if the person being asked out, turns down the date and then turns out to be a below average worker and deserves a below-average pay raise and performance appraisal. What will the person (manager) who asked that worker out do? If he/she gives the worker the below average raise and performance appraisal, that worker may complain that he/she was only given that because he/she turned down a request for a date. If he/she gives the worker a better raise and performance evaluation than is deserved, it could take money out of the pocket of a more deserving employee. And what if that person's supervisor knows that the worker is below average and questions the raise and evaluation? People are not stupid. Your supervisor, like Frida (of ABBA), will know that there is something going on (sorry, I just like the song, "I Know There Is Something Going On" by Frida). Therefore, asking out a co-worker whose pay raise and/or job performance you control, is not only sexual harassment, but will put you in a very difficult position at work and could easily lead to management questioning your judgment.

Now, let's go back to something else I wrote. The act of asking someone whose pay and/or job performance you control is sexual harassment even if the person says yes (and means it). Let's say you two are dating and everything is going well. As much as you may try to hide that fact at work, it will become known. When it comes time for that person's performance review you give him/her a great review because he/she truly earned it. In fact he/she is doing so well that he/she gets a promotion to a new job that comes with higher pay and better benefits. Your supervisor knows how well that person is performing, and is the one who pushed for him/her to get the promotion. You feel good. You have clean hands. However, your dating partner's co-workers will not know how well the person you are dating is doing on the job. It is not their role to monitor his/her work. They have no idea how your dating partner's work stacks up against their own. All they know is that someone was "dating the boss" and now that someone has a promotion. They won't know that is was your supervisor's decision. This has many consequences. First, it makes you look bad, that getting ahead is a social decision, not a business decision. Second, your partner will be looked at as someone who "slept his/her way to the top." In this case it was clear that that didn't happen. However, that matters little.

Worst of all is that your relationship with the co-worker becomes sexual harassment to your dating partner's co-workers. They feel that to get ahead in their workplace they have to "date" their supervisor. Remember, sexual harassment is about power and control. They observed a situation where someone who in their eyes is "sleeping with the boss", a person in a position of power over their raises and performance appraisals, promoted a person he/she was "sleeping with."

(5) If you are the person being asked out by someone who controls your pay and/or your job performance, know that you are being sexually harassed and you have the option of bringing it up with personnel (Human Resources), or more senior management. You can also just deal with that person one-on-one to let him/her know what he/she has done. Of course my selfish preference is that you buy him/her a copy of this book, with paperclips on the pages dealing with this issue, and the appropriate text highlighted, and hand it to him/her. How you react depends upon what makes you feel most comfortable.

Social life at work worksheet

Have you ever dated and then broke up with someone who you worked with, or who lived in the same building, or was a next door neighbor?

1. Yes   No

2A. If yes; using the instance where the break up was the worst, how comfortable was it for you immediately after the break up while at work or at home?

2B. If yes; using the instance where the break up was the worst, how comfortable do you believe it was for the other person immediately after the break up while at work or at home?

_____

_____

3A. If no; if it was a bad break-up, how comfortable do you believe it would have been for you immediately after the break up while at work or at home if that person lived next door to you or worked next to you?

_____

_____

3B. If no; if it was a bad break-up, how comfortable do you believe it would have been for the other person immediately after the break up while at work or at home if that person lived next door to you or worked next to you?

_____

_____

EXERCISE WB7

Marie works for Phil. They find out they have a lot in common and start dating. They try to keep their relationship hidden because there are rules against a supervisor dating one of his or her employees. One day, Gene catches them making out in the parking lot and soon Joyce does as well. Soon after, Marie gets a promotion.

Q1. What problem could this cause for Marie with her coworkers?

_____

_____

_____

_____

_____

_____

_____

_____

_____

_____

_____

_____

Q2. Statement – If a supervisor makes sexual advances to a willing employee; that could still be considered sexual harassment because others in the company might construe that as something the supervisor favors when it comes to giving raises and promotions. Do you agree or disagree with this statement. Please support your answer.

Q3. If Marie was hired on merit, then Phil and Marie break up, and later the job proves to be too much for her, and for the betterment of the company Phil needs to replace her; why might Phil be reluctant to do so?

*****

ESOL EXERCISE WB14

Q1. A reflexive pronoun occurs when the subject of a sentence is the exact same as the object of a sentence. Which sentence below uses a reflexive pronoun?

   A. Should I limit myself to dating people outside of my workplace?
   B. I want to be successful at work.
   C. I will not date anyone at work.
   D. I want to be successful at work, so I will limit myself to dating people outside of my workplace.

Q2. Re-write Work Readiness Exercise WB7, Q3 as a series of three **what if** questions.

_____

_____

_____

_____

_____

_____

Q3. Write one **what about** question that could be asked based on the content in the short write-up for Work Readiness Exercise WB7.

_____

_____

_____

_____

*****

Your Employment Relationship

All teams have team rules. Some may make sense to you, some may not, but you have to follow them all. For example, Tom Coughlin who has coached the Jacksonville Jaguars and New York Giants, had a rule that players had to be five minutes early to team meetings or they would be considered late and fined. Early in his coaching **stint** with the Giants, one of the team's best players and team leaders, Michael Strahan, got angry because he was on time for the official start of a team meeting, but was not there five minutes early and was fined.

While many of the Giant players did not understand the rule, I did. Coughlin was trying to instill a workplace behavior in the players. That behavior is that in order to ensure that you are not late for an event; you need to plan to get there early. You do not plan to get there at the exact moment the event is starting. Let's say that in Coughlin's case he was starting off his meeting by talking about his defensive game plan for the next game, and Strahan, a key player on defense, was late. He would be faced with a decision to delay the meeting (throwing off the timing for the whole day), start the meeting and then re-start again when Strahan showed up, or catch Strahan up when the meeting was over. None of these options is ideal and all cause work delays.

This brings up another point. Just because you may feel that a rule does not make sense, there is almost always a legitimate reason for the rule. Often management will not explain the reason for the rule because they believe it will be too time consuming to explain their reasoning to everyone, or they do not do want to get into a debate about a rule they feel strongly about.

Your new team (your employer) therefore has team rules. So get a copy of the team rules, called the Employee Handbook, read it and ask your Supervisor or Human Resources Manager questions if you do not understand something in the Employee Handbook. Some small businesses do not have a formal book. They may have memos stating workplace rules, or the rules may be informal and passed on verbally.

In some instances the rules will not be told directly to new employees. The new employee will be expected to use common sense and observe the workplace to understand and follow the rules for their employer. If you find yourself in this situation, do not assume; ask questions. The best person to ask is your supervisor. You can ask your co-workers, but if they are confused about a rule or do not know a rule, you cannot use that as an excuse if you do something wrong by following your co-worker's wrong information. There are situations where your Supervisor will pair you up with a co-worker and tell you to learn from him/her. That is a different situation. Ask that co-worker questions. However, if that co-worker tells you something that does not make sense (even if you like the information such as Fridays you can leave two hours early if you finish your work), check with your Supervisor to be sure the information is correct.

There are no cases where businesses have no work rules! So you must know, understand, and follow the rules to be considered a valuable member of the team (your employer).

Some common topics found in Employee Handbooks are listed below. If you do not know the "rules" in your place of business regarding these topics, ask questions to find out what the rules are.

Employee Benefits

Topics may include medical insurance, vacation time, holidays, sick days, personal days, pension plans, life insurance, tuition reimbursement, workers compensation insurance, disability, etc.

Company Policies

Topics may include sexual harassment, discrimination, dating in the workplace, substance abuse, drug testing, smoking, leave of absence, severe weather, maternity leave, death in family leave, equal opportunity employer, reporting workplace accidents, use of company property for personal use, employee discounts, gifts from customers, confidential information, visitors, employees selling their own products in the workplace, employees holding a second job, grievances with co-workers/supervisors, employee discipline (suspension, termination), etc.

Compensation

Topics may include wage and salary schedules, performance appraisals, raises, promotions, overtime, pay periods, payroll deductions, tips, etc.

Employee Workplace Rules

Topics may include reporting times, attendance, punctuality, workplace safety, dress code, handling customer records, computer use, copier use, telephone etiquette, customer service, email etiquette, personal decorum in the workplace (no joking around, no arguing, etc.), problem resolution process, lunch, breaks, eating at your work station, etc.

Improve your skills to become more valuable to your employer

As an asset in the workplace, you are just like a stock on the Stock Exchange. If a company comes out with a great new product idea, one that will take the market by storm, you might be tempted to purchase that stock based on the potential of the new product. However, for that stock price to increase the company would have to make the product, introduce it to the marketplace; and then the product would have to perform as advertised. If not the stock price may not only fail to increase, but could decline.

The same concept is true in the workplace. You are hired based on the company's expectations. You need to meet those expectations to keep your job. To meet expectations, you will be expected to not only utilize the skills and knowledge indicated on your resume, but to learn how to apply them to the specific tasks you will be performing on your job. You will also be expected to be a positive influence in the workplace. To get a promotion, you may have to increase your skill and knowledge base (e.g. learning Excel and Access) and/or learn how to perform more complex functions at work (e.g. how to operate more complex machines so you can fill in when a co-worker is absent) and/or display abilities required of employees at higher job levels in the company (e.g. good leadership skills).

As you continue to add to your skill and knowledge base both on and off the job, your value to the company increases. So your "personal employee stock price" increases. As your "employee stock price" increases, your compensation (wages/salary plus benefits) increases as well.

Therefore, you <u>must</u> continue to learn on and off the job, if you want to grow your pay significantly. After all, as Simon and Garfunkel sang, "I am a Stock, I am an Island", or something like that.

Learning strategy

There are steps you can take to ensure that you continue to learn, which continues to make your "employee stock price" rise. They are:

- ✓ <u>Make learning a priority</u> – when given an opportunity to learn something new, take it, always. You never know when it will come in handy and it improves your value as an employee.
- ✓ <u>Seek out opportunities to learn</u> – be proactive, whether enrolling in courses, volunteering for new assignments at work, offering to become a co-worker's emergency backup, etc.; the more you learn, the more valuable you become.
- ✓ <u>Have a plan for learning</u> – set learning objectives (what you want to learn), research the best ways to obtain that skill/knowledge, and follow through and learn.
- ✓ <u>Remain enthused and motivated</u> – learning new skills and knowledge can be difficult, don't give up, stay focused and don't be afraid to ask for help during the learning process.
- ✓ <u>Know that learning is for you first, your employer second</u> – whenever you are given an opportunity (or even required) to learn, realize that you are helping yourself by increasing your "employee stock price" and if you leave that company, you take your higher "employee stock price" with you.
- ✓ <u>Approach everything new as an opportunity to learn and increase your value</u> – always be observant and ask questions. When someone at work is explaining how he/she performs a work task, don't "zone out"; listen carefully to what is being said, and learn how that task is done. If you do not understand something ask questions.
- ✓ <u>Do not limit what and where you learn</u> – you can learn on the job, you can learn away from work (e.g. ask a friend to show you how to use a computer program), you can learn at a community education program, you can learn at a school, you can even learn at

social events. When someone in a higher position than you talks about his/her work and how he/she received a promotion, don't think of that person as boastful, or talking down to you, or self-centered (even if true); think of it as an opportunity to learn something that can increase your "employee stock price." Who cares why that person is saying what he/she is saying, just see if he/she is saying anything useful for your career.

✓ <u>Do not limit learning to work-related topics</u> – have you heard of the big sale that takes place on the golf course? This happens. Therefore, learn everything you can. For example, knowing current events could help you appear to be a more rounded person and that could be important if you were trying to get promoted to a job that included representing your company at social events.

✓ <u>Learn about yourself</u> – by looking objectively at who you are, you will be able to identify areas where you need to improve and find ways to learn to improve, so you can grow your "employee stock price."

A true story about raises

Let me share with you something that one of my new employees once said to me and how I responded.

He said, "I have been here a month and a half and I've been doing a really good job, so where is my raise?"

I responded, "You have been doing a really good job, thanks. But do you think I hired you to do a bad job? Or, maybe, that I hired you to do just an okay job? For the record, I hired you, and am paying you, to do a really good job. So since you are doing what I hired you to do, I'll let you keep your job."

I said the last sentence with a smile (positive personal signal) since at that point I was teasing him a bit. But I made my point to him, and hopefully to you. You are being paid to do a good job so do not expect extra rewards for doing what you are being paid to do. In my real life case, I then went on to explain to him the process and timetables for raises and informed him that if he kept up his performance, he could expect a nice raise at the appropriate time.

Raises

Raises usually come at specific times. Most often it is related to how long you have been working for the company. The most common timeframe is a year, hence the term "annual raise." Performance appraisals usually come before a raise. In fact, what is written on the performance appraisal often helps determine the amount of the raise. While this is the usual "rule of thumb," some companies do have different timeframes (for example: every 6 months, specific dates tied to the calendar, dates tied to personal accomplishments such as passing a test or obtaining a degree, etc.).

Raises usually have two components. The first is cost of living. This is a portion of the raise given to help offset increases in day-to-day living. This amount is often based on economic data, and not company data. The second part of the raise is performance based. This is the portion of your raise that is based on how well you are doing in your job (often as written in your performance appraisal). In some companies there are policies in place that employees with very bad performance appraisals are not even eligible for cost of living increases.

Keep in mind that some businesses, especially ones with unions, have predetermined raises. Unions often negotiate the timing and amount of raises and promotions. This is like a pass-fail evaluation rather than a test where you can get an A,B,C, etc. If you meet the job qualifications, personal qualifications, and job performance, you get a predetermined (union negotiated) pay increase. If you work for a union, find out the rules on raises and promotions so you can put yourself in a position to get raises and promotions.

Percent versus amount

Raises can be given as either dollar amounts or a percent increase over your existing pay. Dollar amount raises are straight forward, but often difficult to do because cost of living increases (to account for increases in every day life costs such as gas and food) varies by person. So if cost of living is said to have gone up by 2%, many businesses give a 2% cost of living increase as part of their employees' annual raises.

However, when employers account for cost of living and use percent raises, employees who exchange information on the amount of their raises (which you should not do because most people will lie about how much their raise was anyway), may come away confused. For example an employee with a very good performance appraisal may appear to have received a lower raise than an employee with an average performance appraisal. This is because of the cost of living factor and the nature of percents.

For example:

Alan has worked for the company for 25 years and is earning $60,000 and has an employee performance rating of fair.

Nancy has worked for the company for 3 years and is earning $40,000 and has an employee rating of excellent.

With a 3% cost of living increase and a 2% performance increase, Alan gets a 5% raise which equals $3,000.

With a 3% cost of living increase and a 4% performance increase (double the percentage Alan received), Nancy gets a 7% raise which equals $2,800.

If Alan and Nancy compared the amounts of their raises, Alan, the fair employee got $200 more than Nancy, the excellent employee.

This was only because Alan has been with the company much longer, so his salary was higher; making his lower percent raise result in more money than the higher percent raise that Nancy received.

As far as the company was concerned, Nancy received double the performance raise (4% vs. 2%) that Alan received.

So even if you compare raises and everyone is telling the truth, you have to know all factors before just looking at the dollar amount of the raise.

Promotions

Except when promotions are based on specific credentials, which is the exception not the rule, promotions can only occur when there is a job opening in the company.

A promotion occurs when an employee in a company is given a new job assignment that is considered a job function with more responsibility and a higher pay scale than that employee's current job.

If there are no open jobs at a higher level in the company than the job you are performing, there is no opportunity for a promotion for you.

In addition, many promotions are outside of your supervisor's work area. That means your supervisor can recommend you, but he/she is not the person making the decision on whether or not you get the job. It is the person you are interviewing with.

ESOL EXERCISE WB15

Q1. What is the meaning of the word stint in bold in the first paragraph of this chapter?

    A. audition
    B. success
    C. period of work
    D. failure

Q2. What is meant by compare and contrast?

    A. Identifying what is the same between two different items or statements.
    B. Identifying what is true and what is false about a statement.
    C. Identifying what is true and what is false between two different items or statements.
    D. Identifying what is the same and what is different between two different items or statements.

Q3. What was the lesson learned in *A true story about raises*?

    A. You are hired to do a good job; that is the expectation of your employer; so do a good job to earn the money you are being paid.

    B. If you are doing a good job, that is going above and beyond and you deserve a raise; so ask for a raise.

    C. Even if you are doing a good job, never ask for a raise.

    D. It doesn't matter how well you perform your job, you will be paid anyway.

*****

Employee stock price worksheet

List three things you can learn (or continue learning) that will help you become more valuable to your employer; hence improve your chances of increasing your pay.

1. _____

2. _____

3. _____

ESOL *Employee stock price worksheet add-on*

1. When called on by the instructor, inform the class of the type of job you have or are looking for and your three choices listed in the *Employee stock price worksheet*. Also explain why you chose the three items (how they make you more valuable in your current/hoped for job).

2. The instructor will choose two individuals who have talked about the same or similar jobs and identified different things to learn to make them more valuable to their employer. The instructor will then facilitate a class discussion comparing and contrasting the two approaches. Everyone needs to participate in this discussion.

EXERCISE WB8

Q1. What is the difference between a raise and a promotion?

_____
_____
_____
_____

Q2. What are the reasons for raises?

_____
_____
_____
_____

Q3. What are the reasons for promotions?

_____
_____
_____
_____
_____

Q4. What can you do to put yourself in position for a promotion?

_____
_____
_____
_____
_____

Q5. Does getting a better raise than another worker always mean that that worker will receive more money than the other worker?

_____
_____
_____
_____
_____

*****

EXERCISE WB9

Q1. Using the information that follows; who would you promote to support person? Explain why you chose that person.

Let's say you are the supervisor of a work unit that has six phone representatives and one support person. The support person earns more money than the phone representatives because he/she has to know Microsoft Excel and Microsoft Access.

The support person generates management reports that you read and analyze. It is your insightful analysis that is going to help you go far and earn big bucks in the company. The "big boss" has been very impressed with your analysis of the data in the reports.
One of the reasons you are able to write insightful analyses is because your support person is a whiz at generating custom Excel and Access reports that helps organize the data that you analyze.

Then your support person leaves the company. Your supervisor says because the call volume is down, that you need to promote one of the phone representatives to the job of support person. The phone representative staff will now be down to five.

You look at your six phone representatives to determine who should get the promotion to support person.

- Person 1 has a performance rating of excellent, and has no computer experience.
- Person 2 has a performance rating of very good, and has no computer experience.
- Person 3 has a performance rating of good, and has some experience in Excel and Access.
- Person 4 has a performance rating of good, and has no computer experience.
- Person 5 has a performance rating of fair, and has no computer experience.
- Person 6 has a performance rating of poor, and knows Excel and Access very well.

Person number to promote: _____

Explanation:

_____
_____
_____
_____
_____
_____
_____
_____
_____
_____
_____
_____
_____
_____
_____
_____
_____
_____
_____
_____
_____

*****

Please note that as the supervisor, you were aware of all the facts presented here; as one of the phone representatives (worker, not a supervisor) you probably wouldn't be. Just understand that there are many factors that determine who gets promoted. While management wants to reward a deserving employee, the key is to place someone in the job that will perform it well.

Program Wrap-Up

Now, after completing this course, perform the same exercise that you did for the Program Prep.

Write a three paragraph essay explaining what the term "workplace basics" means to you. The first paragraph should introduce the topic (purpose of the three paragraph write-up) and contain a couple of sentences regarding your definition of "workplace basics." The second paragraph should contain some specific behaviors and or skills that help illustrate your definition (what an employee needs to do to ensure that he or she performs "workplace basics" up to the standards of his or her supervisor). The third paragraph should have a conclusion regarding why workplace basics are important to employers.

_____

_____

_____

_____

_____

_____

_____

_____

_____

_____

_____

_____

_____

_____

_____

Q2. Write a paragraph comparing and contrasting your views on workplace basics from before the class (your Program Prep write-up) and after the class (the write-up you just completed in Program Wrap-Up).

_____

_____

_____

_____

_____

_____

_____

_____

_____

_____

_____

_____

_____

_____

_____

_____

_____

_____

_____

_____

Q3. When called on, choose one of the items in your second paragraph, inform the class what it is, why it is important, and how your view on that topic has changed (or has not changed) after taking this course. Whenever possible, use an item that has not been discussed previously.

Certification Scenarios

Workplace Basics Scenario 1

Jerry works for the company If It Wasn't True It Would Be Funny, Inc. Every day something goes wrong. In fact, most days, many things go wrong. However, that isn't the worst part. It's the way the people that work at the company react to these events. It's like they have had no training in basic workplace skills.

Today, when Jerry stops bye Joe's house to pick him up on his way to work, Joe walks out in his PJs and tells him he forgot to set his alarm, he was out late partying last night and was going to blow off the day by calling in sick rather than coming in late. Jerry reminds him that this is an important day since they have a lot of work to do to be sure that they fulfill Much Ado About Nothing's order by the end of the day. Joe just smiles and says, "That's their problem, it has no impact on me." Jerry then chips in, "Isn't this your seventh sick day this year? We only get six." Joe shrugs and says, "I don't know how many sick days we get." Oh, Jerry thinks that crazy Joe D.

When Jerry arrives at work, 10 minutes early, he is pleased to see that Carol is already at her desk busy working. Carol, a new mother, looks alert. Like him, Carol takes her job very seriously. Jerry greets her by asking, "how's the new baby?' Carol responds, "Fine, thanks. Our regular daycare provider cancelled at the last minute so I had to drop her off at my mom's on the way to work. Jerry, you have to come out and see the baby." Jerry, responds, "My weekends are pretty booked, but from the pictures I can see she's breathtaking."

For his first task of the day Jerry has to work with Kenny. Kenny thinks he's a funny guy. He is always telling jokes, many of which use curses and are sexual in nature. Not only does Jerry find the jokes in bad taste, but he finds Kenny's "comedy act" in general very unfunny. Worse, Kenny doesn't believe in using deodorant so working with him is a challenge to the senses. Jerry often finds himself rushing through his work when paired with Kenny. Today, he notices the plant supervisor, Russell, watching Kenny very closely. During his last performance review with Russell, Jerry's only negative comment came in regards to the work he performed with Kenny. Russell commented that Jerry's work was a little sloppy when working with Kenny and he was surprised because, otherwise, his work was near perfect. When Jerry mentioned this to Carol, she said that she received the exact same feedback from Russell regarding her work with Kenny.

After Jerry finishes his work with Kenny, Russell calls him over and gives him a new assignment. Russell tells him that the company expects an OSHA audit sometime in the next few weeks and he is giving Jerry a special task. He wants Jerry to walk around the plant and note unsafe conditions and practices. This is the assignment Jerry hoped to get. There is an opening in the company for a Safety Supervisor and Jerry took an OSHA training course at night to help put him in a position to get that job. It appears, given that Russell assigned him this task, that management has taken notice.

As soon as Jerry starts his safety tour, he observes that no one is using the machine affectionately nicknamed Kramer. Jerry then asks one of the workers why the machine isn't being used. The worker informs Jerry that the machine is out of order, so if used, it could be dangerous. Jerry then asks the worker, "How does everyone know not to use that machine?" He tells Jerry that everyone on the floor has been notified not to use the machine. So Jerry follows up with, "What if someone forgets; and what about next shift?" The worker responds; "That's their problem, not mine." Ah, Jerry thinks, what else should I expect from (making a fist with his right hand), Newman. Okay, Jerry thinks, this is problem number one.

At the far corner of the room Jerry notices a frayed cord attached to the fax machine. Elaine is standing next to the fax machine drinking water she got from the water cooler. Immediately, Jerry remembers Elaine telling him that their supervisor, Russell, asked her out on a date. Elaine turned him down flat, but you could tell Russell was still pinning after her.

In a flash, someone rushes past Elaine and bumps her elbow causing her to spill her water. As the water is making its way towards the frayed cord, Elaine, enraged, chases the person who bumped her elbow shouting, "Come back here. If you think I'm going to clean that up, think again." Jerry notes this as problem number two.

Jerry continues his walking tour and enters the break room. There he notices his good friend George banging on the candy machine because, George says, the machine took his money and didn't give him his candy bar. Right next to the candy machine is a garbage can. Above the garbage can is a fire extinguisher with the label A,B,C. Jerry next witnesses George throwing his lit cigarette into the garbage can. The only thing in the can besides the cigarette is one piece of paper. Smoke immediately starts to rise from the garbage can. George, noticing the smoke, runs out of the room yelling, "Fire, fire." Jerry notes this as problem number three.

Jerry then starts to walk back to his work station. Doing so, he passes through the work shop again where he notices Puddy working. Puddy has band aids all over his fingers. Puddy is using a machine that has very rough surfaces. Jerry further notices that Puddy is not wearing protective gloves. That's why Puddy has all those cuts. So Jerry asks Puddy why he is not wearing gloves. Puddy tells him, "Wearing the gloves is optional." Jerry looks again at Puddy's hands and says, "Soon your hands will be so cut up you won't be able to work; and still you don't wear gloves?" Puddy responds simply, "That's right. " Then adds, "That's what Worker's Comp is for." Jerry shakes his head and moves on. This time Jerry thinks a policy needs to be changed.

As Jerry approaches his work station he falls and bangs his head resulting in a large cut (laceration) with lots of bleeding. As Jerry is being taken from the room by the ambulance crew he sees Cosmo cleaning up his blood spill using his bare hands. Boy, Jerry thinks, even as I'm going to the hospital I see a fifth problem.

Workplace Basics Scenario 2

It is Louie's first day on a new job. On his way to work he runs into traffic and a drive that took him 25 minutes when he came in for an interview, takes him 50 minutes because of the traffic. The result is that he gets into work at 8:25 AM instead of his scheduled time of 8:00 AM. He explains what happened with the traffic to his new boss, who asks, "What road do you take to work?" Louie responds, "I95." His boss then counters with, "I95 is always backed up this time in the morning on work days." Louie replies, "Geez, I'm sorry." His boss just walks away.

When Louie meets with Human Resources his first task is to fill out paperwork for his benefits. When finished, he is handed the company's Employee Handbook. The head of Human Resources then tells him to read the Handbook while she gets his benefits paperwork processed.

She returns in 30 minutes and asks Louie if he read the manual. He didn't, but he answers, "Yes," thinking he could read it at another time. She then asks if he has any questions. Louie answers, "No."

So the head of Human Resources picks up the book, turns to the first page, and notices that Louie did not sign the form indicating that he read and understood the Handbook. She asks him why he didn't sign that form. Louie answers, "I forgot. I'll sign it now."

Before handing the Handbook back to Louie, the head of Human Resources makes it clear that if Louie doesn't understand anything in the Handbook, please, let's discuss it now.

Louie, with impatience clearly coming through in his response answers, "Just give me the Handbook so I can sign the form."

The Head of Human Resources gives the Handbook back to Louie, who signs the form stating he read and clearly understands everything in the Handbook, while clearly knowing that he never read the book.

Louie is then taken to his new office. It is a cubicle (temporary, free-standing walls). His cubicle is in the middle of the room and has walls that are four feet high, high enough to give him privacy when seated at his desk, and low enough for his supervisor (and others) to see into his cubicle when walking past it. On the wall of the cubicle he hangs the Sports Illustrated swimsuit calendar.

He then notices that his cubicle is next to Latka, who is from the Caspiar. Louie is a patriot and does not want to work next to an immigrant. He immediately sends an email to his new boss asking to be moved as far away from that guy as possible. In fact, that reminds him of a cartoon joke he has in his briefcase. It is poking fun at Muslims, but there is no bad language, and even has a hidden dig at Jewish people. Louie walks over to the copier and makes 20 copies and puts them in all the employee mailboxes on this floor.

Later in the day Louie walks over to Elaine's desk. He has been meaning to introduce himself to her all day. Elaine is Louie's assistant. He controls her pay raises and writes her performance appraisal. The first thing Louie notices is that he finds her very attractive. The second thing he notices is that she has an engagement ring on, but no wedding ring. Louie asks her about her wedding plans. When he hears she has no firm plans, Louie tells her that she should go on a date with him just once, and she will never set a wedding date. When she turns him down, he somewhat kiddingly reminds her he is in charge of her raises and performance reviews so maybe she should reconsider.

Before leaving for the day, Louie is introduced to Simka, a co-worker at the same job level as Louie himself. Simka was told to meet with Louie by her supervisor to tell him about the client he will be serving. It was Simka's client but she has been overloaded since taking on Alex's clients, the person Louie was hired to replace. Boy, Louie thinks, Simka is really cute. After talking about the client, Simka is set to leave for the day. She extends her hand to shake Louie's hand goodbye, but instead Louie says, "come on, we're going to be working closely on this account for awhile, I think a hug goodbye is in order." He then gives Simka a hug.

When Louie comes in the next day he sees a note on his desk telling him to report to his supervisor's office at 8:00 AM. Louie looks at his watch and it indicates that the time is 8:25 AM. There was traffic on I95 again so it took Louie 50 minutes to get work. On his way to his supervisor's office Louie stops bye Elaine's desk, winks and asks, "Given any more thought to our date?" and then thinks, this is going to be a wonderful day.

When Louie gets to his supervisor's office he sees that the head of Human Resources is there along with Simka.

Louie knocks on the door and immediately his supervisor asks him why he wasn't at his office at 8:00 AM.

Maybe this isn't going to be such a wonderful day in the life of Louie after all.

About the Author

Jay Goldberg, MBA, is a former Service Director for Citibank. At Citibank, Mr. Goldberg specialized in customer service management, measurement, training, capacity planning, profitability, MIS reporting, and strategic planning.

After almost fourteen years with Citibank, Mr. Goldberg left to form his own consulting firm, DTR Inc. DTR Inc. specializes in writing business plans, developing workplace training programs, designing and implementing customer service strategies, performing strategic planning and market research (e.g., surveys, focus groups, etc.), helping businesses build their brands, and training managers and employees.

At DTR Inc., Mr. Goldberg developed the program parameters, program strategy, curriculum, lesson plans, assessments, competency statements, and certification tests for a Work Readiness Training Program called the best Work Readiness Certification Program in the United States by a representative of the National Skills Standard Board at a presentation of the Program in Jacksonville, Florida on 01/13/03.

Mr. Goldberg later updated, modified and added to that Program for a second client and wrote a book, "How to Get, Keep and Be Well Paid in a Job" (ISBN = 9781432725297), specifically tailored to individuals looking to improve their work readiness skills.

In 2007, Mr. Goldberg was instrumental in helping the Palm Beach County Resource Center develop a revolutionary Entrepreneurship Training Program. The program's structure was unlike any other in the marketplace, and would prove to be highly successful.

In 2012, Mr. Goldberg's entrepreneurship book, "Building a Successful Business," (ISBN = 9781470000639) was published. The book is now being used as a textbook for entrepreneurship courses. The book is both a textbook and a workbook with tools entrepreneurs can use to help start, grow and manage their businesses.

While at the Palm Beach County Resource Center, Mr. Goldberg worked with hundreds of small businesses and got a good handle on how to best structure and implement a work readiness training program to ensure that the benefits of training would be demonstrated in the workplace.

In 2013 Mr. Goldberg published his book for his comprehensive work readiness and customer service training program. There is a teacher book, a classroom book (without answers) and PowerPoint presentations available in the full program.

Contact Mr. Goldberg at Book@DTRConsulting.BIZ. Be sure to write "your work readiness book" in the subject line to ensure that your email is not deleted as junk mail. His business's web site is www.DTRConsulting.BIZ.

BUILDING A SUCCESSFUL BUSINESS
By JAY GOLDBERG

The entrepreneurs' business plan and management skill instruction manual, tip sheet, and workbook

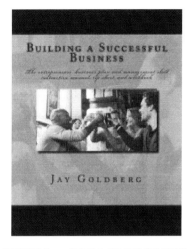

ISBN = 9781470000639

In its first year, about half of all businesses fail. Five years down the line, depending upon which study you look at, only 1 in 10 to 1 in 3 businesses are left standing. The main reasons businesses fail are no business plan and poor management. That is why this book covers both topics.

However, this book goes beyond other books on these topics. The book not only provides a road map for writing a business plan, but also provides a strategy for writing a business plan.

A business plan is both a strategic document and a sales document. It also provides the reader with a look into the skills, knowledge and personality of the business owner. Therefore, a good business plan is written to satisfy all of these uses. In addition, this book provides information on how to research and organize the information needed for a business plan, and has worksheets the entrepreneur can use to help make the process easier.

Likewise, management topics such as strategic planning (SWOT analysis plus), advertising, branding, project management, customer service management, cash flow management, sales skills, business writing and more are explained, and a method is provided for each management skill that can be implemented and used in the business. There are worksheets for many of the management topics as well.

www.createspace.com/3785695

Made in the USA
Middletown, DE
16 August 2018